Foreword

"Mustang How-To Volume 1" is a collection of magazine articles from the early 1980s. The text has been edited slightly for the current printing to clarify information which has changed since the material was first published. In other instances (for example, product prices) original information has been left intact for historical interest.

**Printed and bound
in the United States of America**

MUSTANG HOW-TO VOLUME I

EDITOR
Donald N. Farr

ART DIRECTOR
Howard E. Buck Jr.

PRODUCTION DIRECTOR
Howard E. Buck Jr.

PRODUCTION ASSISTANTS
L. Del Sellers, Robert C. Parker

STAFF ARTIST
Robert C. Parker

ISBN 0-9624908-3-0
(Previously ISBN 0-941596-04-4)

**Copyright © 1989 by California
Mustang Sales and Parts, Inc.,
19400 San Jose Ave.,
City of Industry, CA 91748
All rights reserved**

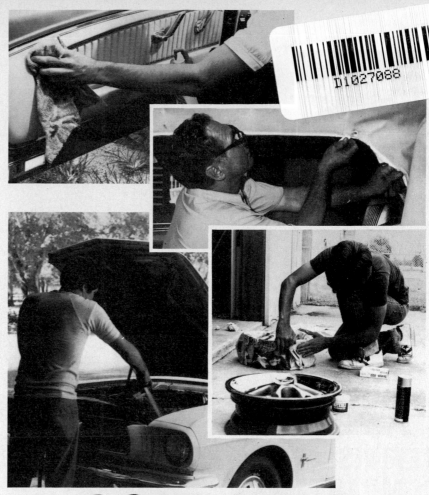

CONTENTS

How To
REFINISH YOUR MUSTANG ENGINE COMPARTMENT

Engine compartments are, by nature, dirty places. They are constantly exposed to all types of engine grime and grease, from minute oil seepages to clouds of blowby spewing from the oil filter caps. From underneath, the area is attacked by every type of filth known to inhabit the earth's highways and freeways, vacuumed up into and onto every crack and crevice within and glued in place forever by the sticky oil residue and blowby. Add an occasional antifreeze bath from a busted hose and corrosion-causing battery acid and you've got quite a mess.

The appearance of an engine and its surrounding area is, quite fortunately in many cases, hidden out of view when the hood is closed. So while the exterior and interior of the car gets washed and cleaned once a week, the engine just sits there in the dark covered with 2 inches of 10 year old grease.

Now a dirty engine in your 1972 Caprice wouldn't make much difference to anyone, but in a Mustang, well, that's a horse of a different color. You expect a nice Mustang to

have a spotless engine compartment. Or at least a clean one. There's nothing worse than showing off your glistening paint and reupholstered interior, then having the admirer ask, "How's it look under the hood?" when you can barely find the dipstick through the sea of oil on top of the motor.

With only a few basic tools, some spray paint, and a couple of spare afternoons, you can revitilize your Mustang's engine compartment to make it look showroom new.

Getting your Mustang's engine compartment back into presentable condition requires less time and effort than you may think. With only a few basic tools, some spray paint, and a couple of spare afternoons or a weekend, you can transform that unsightly area into squeekly clean, showoff-

worthy piece of mechanical equipment.

Our project engine resides within our art director's newly purchased Mustang coupe, a white '66 that spent much of its life in storage. The exterior and interior of the car looked pretty good, considering the amount of time garaged, but the engine compartment, as you can see from the photo, was a complete disaster area. Some previous owner had painted the 200 six cylinder's valve cover a chocolate-colored brown, in contrast to the head and block's oil smeared blue. The leaking radiator was covered with more rust than paint, and the engine compartment walls were splattered with rain-sloshed dirt. A typical 15 year old engine bay.

Before tackling the dirty work, inspect your hoses, spark plug wires, etc. and make note of the items that may need replacing. You'll be removing most of these anyway, so you may as well replace the worn parts. Also, if your radiator needs repairs or cleaning, make an appointment with a radiator shop.

With your shopping list of parts in

hand, head for your favorite parts store and purchase the items needed. You'll also need several cans of Gunk, 2 or 3 cans of Ford blue engine paint (depending on the engine size), 4 cans of black paint (either flat, semi-gloss, or gloss, depending on your preference - the original black was a semi-gloss, but we couldn't find any in spray cans here in Lakeland, so we settled for gloss), fine steelwool, some course and fine sandpaper, a bottle of Fantastik and Armour-All, paint thinner, masking tape, and old newspaper.

The degreasing step can be performed in several ways. A steam cleaner is the best and quickest method of clean the engine and it's compartment, but you can achieve the same results at a spray car wash or even in your driveway with a water hose. With the engine warm, cover the carburetor and distributor with plastic (bread bags work well) and spray on a thick coat of Gunk engine cleaner (the foam type will stick to the parts better). Be sure to spray the firewall and other grime-attaching areas, especially the oil pan, steering linkages, and steering gear. Wait 15 minutes and hose off. You may have to repeat the process on heavy oil deposits, and, in some cases, a brush and/or gasket scraper may be necessary to completely remove all traces.

While the engine is drying, disconnect the battery and begin removing all accessories, brackets, pulleys, fan and alternator, distributor cap and wires, gas and vacuum lines, etc. Drain the radiator, disconnect the hoses, and remove from the car. Small items like pulleys and brackets can be soaked in a bucket of kerosene for additional cleaning. Next, remove the battery, solenoid, regulator, windshield washer resevoir, and all other small items attached to the engine compartment walls. Unbolt the upper shock mounting bolts and remove the shock brackets. Wires should be labeled, disconnected, and laid aside. Unless you possess an ultra-keen memory, keep labeled cans nearby to separate the various nuts, bolts, and screws.

For best results, the valve cover(s) should be removed for additional cleaning. Chipped areas on painted covers can be smoothed over with fine sandpaper. In fact, it's not a bad idea to sand the entire cover to make certain all traces of grease and oil are removed. Use fine steelwool to clean

Our project engine compartment. Note the rusty radiator, by-passed heater hose, and dirty firewall.

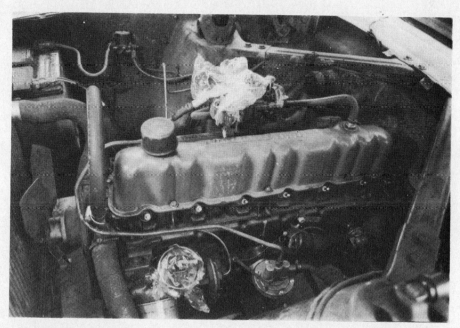

Before spraying on the degreaser/cleaner, cover the carburetor and distributor with Handi-Wrap or plastic bread bags.

chrome and aluminum covers. If possible, have aluminum valve covers sandblasted or glassbeaded. Aluminum intake manifolds can be removed and also glassbeaded, but you'll need a torque wrench to reinstall properly. It's common knowledge that a coat of clear acrylic over glassbeaded aluminum pieces will make them easier to wipe clean, but the clear does tend to turn yellow after a period of time.

It's not necessary to remove every little item from the engine itself, unless you particularly want to.

Smaller or difficult to reinstall parts like the distributor and fuel pump can be easily covered with newspaper and masking tape before painting.

The most tedious step involves masking off the fenders. Everything from the top of the windshield forward should be well covered with newspaper; paint overspray has a nasty habit of sneaking through tiny openings, usually on top of a fender where it can be readily seen. If there's a breeze blowing through your garage or driveway, it's a good idea to cover the rest of the car with a car cover,

After warming up the engine, spray Gunk cleaner everywhere - on the engine, firewall, steering linkages, etc. . . .

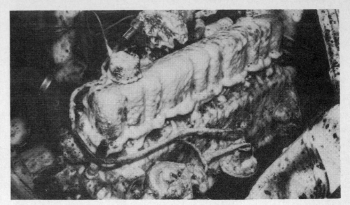

let it stand for approximately 15 minutes . . .

and hose off with a strong stream of water. Repeat if necessary.

Remove all detachable items from the motor and engine compartment. Fan, pulleys, brackets, bolts, etc. can be soaked in kerosene for additional cleaning.

Fuel and vacuum lines should be disconnected and removed or positioned out of the way.

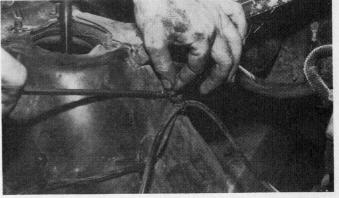

A flat screwdriver can be used to pry open wire hanger straps on the engine compartment and firewall.

old sheets, etc.

Start masking by running a strip of masking tape along the edge of the fender lips, making sure the tape doesn't extend over any of the engine compartment sheetmetal. Take your time during this precedure; the neater the taping, the more detailed the job will look when you've finished. One end of the newspaper can be attached to the top of the tape strip while the other end folds over the fender. Overlap each section of newspaper as you go and completely tape every edge. Follow the same procedure at

the cowl, letting the paper cover the windshield. Spread newspaper over the grille and tape.

Next, grab some 1 page sections of newspaper and wrap the items that will remain unpainted, like the shocks, fuel pump, distributor, etc. The paper can be attached securely with masking tape.

The engine compartment should be painted first since any black overspray that falls on the engine, and there will be plenty, will be covered when the engine is painted. Follow the instructions on the paint

can label, especially heeding the "shake well for 3 minutes" directive. Apply the paint in several thin coats, as opposed to heavy applications which creates runs. Use a sweeping motion to get the paint on evenly. If any hoses or wiring was left inside the compartment, lift them out of the way. Complete the entire engine compartment including the steering linkages, etc., before moving on to the engine.

Now comes the fun part, because, within minutes, your engine will be transformed from a grubby, rusty-

With the accessories out of the way, hidden areas of the engine, usually coated with a thick layer of oil and grease, can be cleaned with an old toothbrush and/or gasket scraper.

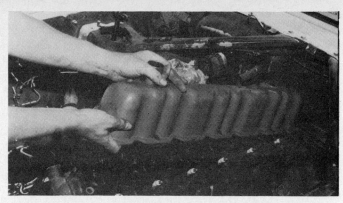

The valve cover(s) should be removed for extra attention.

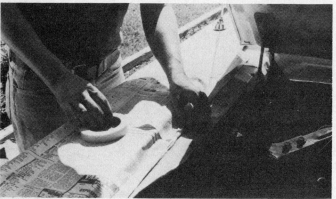

Use care when masking off the engine compartment for paint. This step will be tedious, but the results will be worth the extra time spent.

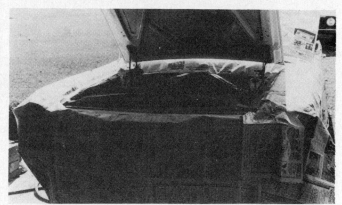

Your Mustang should look like this when the masking is complete.

If you need to complete your project in a short period of time a hair dryer will effectively dry the engine prior to painting.

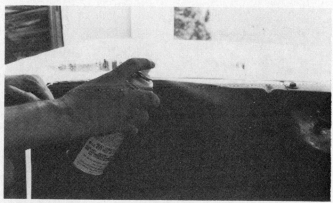

Don't try to rush the painting process. Spray several thin coats as opposed to one or two heavy coats, allowing 10 to 15 minutes between drying time between applications.

Small parts can be spread out on your garage floor or bench for painting.

Be careful during reinstallation - you don't want to chip or mar any freshly painted surfaces.

looking hunk of metal to a vivid blue show-quality motor. The engine paint should be applied in the same manner as the engine compartment black, but you'll have to be more careful - all those bumps and valleys on the engine can cause you to spray too close in some areas.

While the engine paint dries, move on to the accessories and other parts that were removed. The items soaking in the kerosene bucket can be wiped dry, although some heavy grease deposits may need additional cleaning with a kerosene-soaked rag or a wire brush. Sandblasting will really clean the metal pieces, but it's not a necessity on a low-buck refurbishing. Lightly sand the valve covers and air cleaner (unless they're chrome) to prepare for paint.

Spread some newspaper on your garage bench or floor and separate the parts into 2 groups - those to be painted black (brackets, pulleys, fan . . .) and those to be painted blue (air cleaner, valve cover(s) . . .) Again, spray on several thin coats, allowing a few minutes between each application.

The paint will need about 30 minutes to dry, so move to the parts that remain unpainted. Use steelwool to clean the gas and vacuum lines, fuel pumps, distributor, etc. An aluminum/metal polish can be used for additional luster. Wires can be cleaned by pulling them through a cloth soaked with paint thinner.

The condition of your fasteners can add to or detract from the final appearance of your engine refurbishing. Of course, new bolts and screws are the optimum solution, but you can get by just sandblasting or cleaning the old ones. A coat of clear (available in spray cans) will prevent rusting or you can use a small brush to apply high-temperature aluminum paint once the fasteners are installed and tightened.

Reinstall all the engine compartment components and attach their wires and hoses. Then bolt on the valve covers (with new gaskets), intake manifold (if it was removed - be sure to torque the bolts in sequence and to the specifications listed in your shop manual), and the other miscellaneous pieces, taking care not to mar or scratch any of the newly painted surfaces. Slip in the radiator, attach the hoses, and fill with anti-freeze/coolant. Replace the spark plugs if needed and install the

distributor (if removed), distributor cap, and wires. Double-check all clamps on the radiator and heaters hoses before starting the engine - all you need now is anti-freeze all over your fresh paint. Pull off the newspaper and masking tape, stand back, and marvel at your engine's new appearance.

All that's left is the final detailing. Coat all the rubber parts with Armour-All and touch up any scratches or chips that may have occurred during installation. Slap on some new decals and add a sparkling-new radiator cap.

With everything back in place (the correct place, we hope), start the engine. If it spits and coughs while cranking and refuses to start, or starts and idles roughly, check for crossed spark plug wires or incorrect timing (if you pulled the distributor). Once the engine is running, check for any leaks.

Except for a couple of minor details, our Mustang engine compart-

ment project was completed in a day. A defective radiator hose was discovered later and replaced, no doubt only moments before splitting and spraying our pride and joy with sticky green anti-freeze. New decals arrived a few days later, and, with their installation, our project was complete.

Naturally, the more time and effort put into the project will show in the final results. Under ideal circumstances, the Mustang can be left disassembled for a few days while you take your time cleaning, polishing, and detailing, but, if you use the car for everyday transportation, you'll need to complete the project in a hurry. Still, the results can be very satisfying. A frequent washing and touch-up will keep the engine compartment looking new. Never again will you make the excuses for a messy engine. As a matter of fact, you'll probably start making excuses for opening the hood everytime you park - "just checking the oil".

How To
IMPROVE YOUR MUSTANG'S HANDLING

by Paul Duprey

A SWAY BAR PRIMER

This lesson in sway bar selection is aimed at Mustangers who enjoy the finer aspects of handling, whether it be for quick street driving, autocrossing, road racing, or whatever. Also, I hope to put a popular sway bar misconception to rest.

All Mustangs are equipped with a front sway bar, either 5/8, 3/4, 7/8, or 15/16 in diameter, and some came from the factory with a rear bar, 1/2, 5/8, or 3/4 in diameter. The 5/8 front bar is by far the most common found on '65-70 Mustangs since it was part of the standard suspension. Larger front bars were relegated to certain optional handling packages and performance oriented Mustang models like the G.T.s, Mach 1s, Boss 302s, etc.

One common practice used to improve the handling of Mustangs is the installation of the 1 inch diameter Shelby bar. Unfortunately, this addition alone doesn't enhance the Mustang's biggest handling problem — understeer, which occurs when the front tires lose traction before the rear tires when cornering (creating a "pushing" situation). Oversteer is the direct reverse, caused by the rear tires losing traction first. Neutral handling is the fine line that separates the two.

Another term to remember is balance, meaning the ratio of front suspension torsional stiffness to rear suspension torsion stiffness. "Torsional stiffness" is the suspension's ability to combat body lean and roll.

I know, most of you are saying that that's what the 1 inch front sway bar does — prevent roll. But remember, to fight understeer, we need balance. You see, when most people think about improving their suspension with stiffer springs and a larger sway bar, they almost always mean the front suspension. And that is where the problem lies. If you remember only one thing from this course, let it be this — adding more torsional stiffness or roll resistance to the front suspension ADDS MORE UNDERSTEER! Adding additional stiffness to the rear suspension REDUCES UNDERSTEER! The ideal situation falls in the middle — neutral handling.

Look at Table A. It compares the different size sway bars as far as torsional stiffness is concerned. For the sake of comparison, we'll use the figure of 100% as the stiffness of the smallest front and rear bars. It will help you see the added roll resistance of each larger size bar.

Now we get back to what we call "balance". Table B shows the "balance ratio" or "front to rear torsional stiffness ratio" between the different sway bar combinations. Look at the ratio for the

standard suspension's 5/8 bar with no rear bar. The front to rear ratio is 3.12, meaning the front has much more stiffness than the rear. And a stock Mustang like this would understeer like there was no tomorrow.

Now let's do what many people do and add the 1 inch front bar. What's the ratio now? That's right - 5! The larger the number, the more understeer. The average small block Mustang weighing in at about 3,000 pounds needs a ratio in the area of 1.4 to 1.5 to approach a neutral attitude while cornering. Increasing the rear roll stiffness tunes in more oversteer into the rear suspension, which in turn helps cancel out understeer. So, the smaller the ratio, the more pronounced the transition to oversteer.

Another consideration to keep in mind when selecting sway bars is just how much of a good street ride you'd want to sacrifice for the sake of handling. Because as the bars get bigger, the ride gets tougher. Let's say you drive a Sunday-only, or possibly a go-to-work Mustang, and you'd like to keep the decent ride, yet still be able to take those expressway ramps, or that certain back road, at a pretty good clip. The ratio table shows that the smallest bars nearest the correct ratio are a 3/4 front, with a 1/2 rear, or a 7/8 front and a 5/8 rear. The last combination would be noticeably

rougher in ride quality, but not so much that you wouldn't want to try it. Now, if you were building an autocross car, and your car already had the stiffer front and rear springs, and Koni shocks, the ideal suspension set-up would contain as much roll stiffness as possible combined with a bias toward moderate power-on oversteer. Look at the table again and you'll see a 1 inch front bar with either an 11/16 or 3/4 rear bar, or a 1 1/8 front bar with a 15/16 rear bar, would be the ideal starting points.

Just how you set your car up is up to you. But remember, if you plan to use the car primarily on the street, look at Table A to see just how much stiffer and harsher those big bars would be on the street. But if your objective is competitive autocrossing, don't be overly concerned if you can feel every pebble in the road. Just don't hit any pylons!

A good point to remember for a street driven Mustang that doesn't see any autocrossing or vintage racing is that the lighter the car, the smaller the required bars. That is, a light '65 Mustang can get by on the autocross course with just 3/4 front and 1/2 rear bars, whereas a heavier car like a 1970 Boss 302 that came from the factory with 15/16 front and 1/2 rear bars can use larger bars without affecting the ride quality too adversely.

TABLE A	FRONT BAR		REAR BAR	
	5/8	100%	1/2	100%
	3/4	160%	5/8	167%
	7/8	200%	11/16	179%
	15/16	210%	3/4	212%
	1	226%	15/16	228%
	1 1/8	244%		

TABLE B		REAR BAR DIAMETER					
	Front Bar Diameter	None	1/2	5/8	11/16	3/4	15/16
	5/8	3.12	1.25	1.00	.91	.75	.54
	3/4	3.75	1.50	1.20	1.09	1.00	.79
	7/8	4.38	1.75	1.40	1.27	1.16	.93
	15/16	4.7	1.88	1.50	1.36	1.25	1.00
	1	5	2.00	1.60	1.45	1.33	1.06
	1 1/8	5.62	2.25	1.80	1.63	1.50	1.19

FRONT BARS

MODEL	DIAMETER	PART #
1964½-1966		
170, 200, 260, 289	5/8	C5ZZ-5482-B
RPO Handling Package RPO GT Package 289 Hi-Performance	13/16	C5ZZ-5482-A
GT-350	1	S1MS-5482-A
1967-1968		
200, 289, 302	5/8	C7WY-5482-A
RPO Improved Handling Pkg. 390	3/4	C7ZZ-5482-B
289GT, 302GT, 390, 390GT W/Improved Handling Pkg.	7/8	C7ZZ-5482-C
289GT, 302GT, 390, 390GT W/Maximum Handling Pkg. 428CJ GT-350, GT-500, GT-500 KR	15/16	C9ZZ-5482-E
1969		
200, 250, 302, 351	11/16	C9ZZ-5482-B
RPO Handling Package 390 302GT, 351GT, 390GT Mach 1 w/351, 390 BOSS 302 (before 4-14-69)	7/8	C9ZZ-5482-D
Mach 1 w/428, 428CJ, 428SCJ BOSS 429 428GT	15/16	C9ZZ-5482-E
BOSS 302 (after 4-14-69)	3/4	C9ZZ-5482-C
1970		
200, 250, 302, 351W, 351C	5/8	D0ZZ-5482-A
302, 351W, 351C, w/H.D. Suspension	11/16	C9ZZ-5482-A
302 w/Competition Handling Package	7/8	C9ZZ-5482-D
351W, 351C w/Competition Handling Package Mach 1 (all) BOSS 302, BOSS 429 428CJ, 428SCJ (all models) GT-350, GT-500	15/16	C9ZZ-5482-E
1971		
250, 302, 351C	3/4	D2ZZ-5482-A
351C w/Competition Handling Package 351C, CJ, BOSS 351 Mach 1 429CJ, 429SCJ	7/8	D1ZZ-5482-D
1972-1973		
250, 302, 351-2V 351CJ w/o Competition Handling Package 351 HO (before 9-1-71)	3/4	D2ZZ-5482-A

REAR BARS

MODEL	DIAMETER	PART #
1969		
BOSS 429	3/4	C9ZZ-5A772-A
1970		
Competition Handling Package Except 302 Mach 1, BOSS 302, BOSS 429	1/2	D0ZZ-5A772-A
BOSS 302 (Special T/A Racing Part)	11/16	D0ZX-5A772-B
1971-1973		
Competition Handling Package 351CJ Mach 1 (all)	1/2	D1ZZ-5A772-B
BOSS 351, 351HO	5/8	D1ZZ-5A772-A

Handling is a relative thing — it means different things to different people. That's why the standard model Mustangs weren't barn-burning road racers. They couldn't be. For each person wanting a stiff-suspensioned Mustang, there were probably a hundred who didn't. It wouldn't have made economical sense for Ford to have built an S.C.C.A. champion into every Mustang. That's why the suspension system was always a compromise — it does everything asked of it well, but within reason.

The basic Mustang suspension system was no engineering marvel. In fact, it was designed around the basic Falcon platform, the epitome of simplicity. But even though the Mustang lacked sophistication under the wheelwells, it was still a decently mannered road car. And the optional handling packages, although still simple in nature, gave the Mustang enough competent handling power to make cornering fun. Sway bars played a big part in both the standard and optional handling packages.

The Mustang suspension system is a compromise - it does everything asked of it well, but within reason.

Actually, the term "sway bar" is kind of a misnomer. In reality, the bars increase torsional stiffness in the suspension, or, in simpler terms, increase the suspension's ability to resist body lean or roll.

When the front suspension contains too much stiffness, the effect, while cornering, is this: the rear end lifts, transferring more weight to the outside front tire, the one already carrying the brunt of the cornering force. Increase the rear torsional stiffness (by increasing spring rates and/or adding a rear sway bar) and the weight shifts to the outside rear tire, balancing the work load between the outside tires and enabling both to be more effective.

By now, you should see that sway bars can be a fantastic tool to work with. They can increase the torsional stiffness of the suspension without affecting the spring rates. In other words, you can "spring a car" softly for a smooth boulevard ride, but, with the addition of a moderate diameter front bar and rear bar, effectively reduce understeer and body lean to the point where the car will approach, or attain, that fine line between understeer and oversteer — or, "neutral handling". The result is a car that rides nicely, but corners on the proverbial "rails".

The 1964½ through 1973 Mustangs were equipped with many, many different sway bars. And, if you have ever wondered which bars came on what models, the accompaning list should answer all your inner-most questions.

Didn't know there were so many, did you? Now, don't go running down to your local Ford dealer ranting and raving about a 1969 Boss 429 rear sway bar. They're not available anymore. But don't dispair, not all of these are obsolete, and the ones that are can usually be replaced by a suitable piece from any of a large number of aftermarket manufacturers.

If you own a standard model Mustang with a large front bar, that, as far as you can ascertain, was factory installed, chances are good that your car is equipped with an optional handling package. Later Mustangs with rear sway bars are definitely competition suspension cars. However, there were occasions on the assembly line when the correct bar for a particular model wasn't available (delay in parts delivery from the warehouse, etc.). The assembly line foreman wouldn't halt the entire line just for a sway bar — the car got another size bar instead. And that alone could make for some very interesting combinations. But then, that's one of the reasons Mustangs are so much fun — you never know just what combination will turn up next.

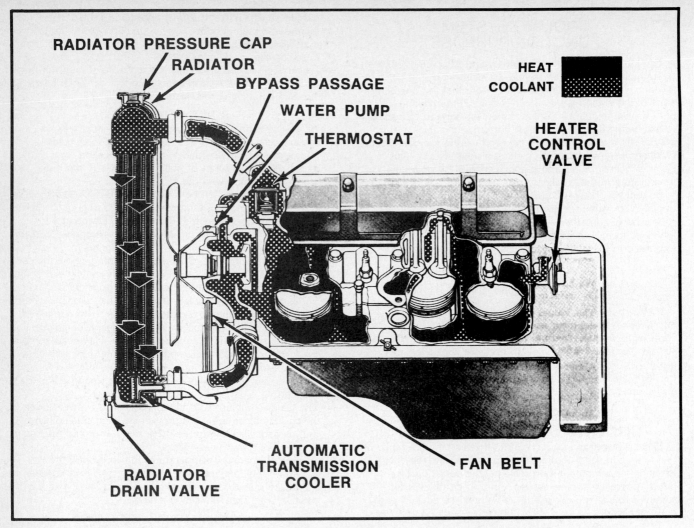

RADIATOR PRESSURE CAP
RADIATOR
BYPASS PASSAGE
WATER PUMP
THERMOSTAT

HEAT
COOLANT

HEATER
CONTROL
VALVE

RADIATOR
DRAIN VALVE

AUTOMATIC
TRANSMISSION
COOLER

FAN BELT

How To
KEEP YOUR MUSTANG RUNNING COOL

Reprinted From Ford's

ENGINES ARE "HEAT MACHINES"

Automotive internal combustion piston engines can be thought of as being basically "heat machines". They cannot develop usable power unless they create heat. And, within certain limits the hotter they run the more efficient they become.

However, only a small part of the heat produced by the burning air-fuel mixture in the combustion chamber — where temperatures often reach over 4000 degrees F. — can be utilized for power output to drive the wheels. Waste heat from combustion and heat generated by friction must be removed.

In a typical water cooled automotive engine approximately one-half the waste heat is removed with the exhaust gas and the other half is removed through the cooling system.

Not well known is the fact that a car's engine dissipates heat by THREE major methods; direct ration to the surrounding air, through the exhaust system, and of course into the cooling system. Roughly 25,000,000 units of heat — often termed BTU's (British Thermal Units) — are dissipated

in 10,000 miles of ordinary driving.

And, as one industry research source claims, heavy driving with a high output engine can reject enough heat energy into a cooling system to melt an average 200 pound engine block in just a few minutes!

Why doesn't the engine just melt into a pool of hot molten metal since cast iron melts around 2500 degrees F., steel gets red hot at around 1500 degrees F. and aluminum melts at about 1200 degrees F.?

Naturally, it is due to the ability of the cooling system to properly handle the tremendous heat load.

To do this, as one example, the water pump of Ford's 240 cubic inch 6-cylinder engine is designed to pump about 696,000 gallons of coolant in 200 hours of operation at an engine speed of 4000 rpm.

Many of the larger V-8 powerplants have pumps that handle even greater volumes than that.

What happens when the engine cooling system is neglected and loses its efficiency?

Common problems that develop whenever metal temperatures are not controlled by proper cooling include pre-ignition, power loss, knock, burned and scored pistons, warped and burned valves, and lubrication failures.

As you can see, cooling systems have a real tough job to do and must do it with a high level of efficiency. Thus, keeping the cooling system at its peak performance requires a complete maintenance tune-up...preferably twice a year.

11

COOLING SYSTEM
FUNCTION/PURPOSE

The job assigned to the cooling system is to remove the waste heat from combustion and the heat generated by friction. However, it is interesting to note that the operating parts of the engine are cooled not only by the cooling system but to some degree by the lubrication system and to a smaller extent by the fuel system. And, not only does the cooling system serve to prevent the heat produced in the combustion chamber from damaging or melting pistons, valves, and cylinder heads, but to also partially control the operating temperature of the crankcase oil.

So you see, the cooling system, operating quietly and unobserved within the confines of metal castings, synthetic rubber hoses, and thin-wall tubing of the radiator, has a major job to perform — a job that many car owners fail to realize is important to the operating efficiency of their engine.

MAINTAINING
COOLING SYSTEM EFFICIENCY

To keep your car's cooling system operating at peak efficiency, the radiator and engine castings must have clean surfaces (both externally and internally) with the other units such as the radiator, thermostat, pressure cap, and water pump performing within the limits designed by the car maker. Fan belt tension must be correct and all hoses must be clean and clamps tight.

EFFECTS OF POOR
COOLING SYSTEM OPERATION

Since it is so important to control the temperature range of the coolant in order to maintain top engine efficiency, let's examine for a moment the problems that develop with a poorly operating cooling system. And no doubt about it, serious damage can occur and you should be advised of the consequences.

RUNNING TOO HOT

• For one thing, an engine operating too hot will cause the engine oil temperature to rise to an excessive heat range and thus form varnish-like deposits on metal parts. These deposits can interfere with the close tolerances in today's engines and upset the efficiency and power output.
• Metal parts that are running to extremes of high temperature because of an overheated cooling system generally cause

burned valves, scored pistons, and damaged bearings.
• Increased oil temperature lowers the oil viscosity and allows it to pass through smaller clearances, therefore contributing to an increase in oil combustion.
• Lowered oil viscosity will also decrease the strength of the oil film and thus lessen main bearing life, camshaft bearing life, and connecting rod bearing life.

RUNNING TOO COLD

• An engine running cold will result in excessive wear of internal operating parts due to the formation of acids, improper running clearances, poor combustion, and an increase in the amount of pollutants sent out into the atmosphere along with the exhaust gases.
• Cylinder wall wear can be EIGHT TIMES GREATER with coolant operating at a temperature of 100 degrees F. or colder as compared with 180 degrees F. temperature. Minimum efficiency of Ford-built engines requires a coolant operating temperature of at least 175 degrees F.
• Operating temperature of an engine running below the car maker's designed level can also cause an equally bad engine lubricating problem, wastes fuel, causes poor performance.
• To illustrate this further, let's examine what happens when fuel is burned in the combustion chamber. The burning of one gallon of fuel produces about one gallon of water — most of it passes out the exhaust system. However, some of the water vapor along with partially burned fuel may blow by the piston rings and into the crankcase. When this happens, the motor oil is diluted and lubricating efficiency is reduced.
• The water combines with the oil and forms a thick sludge which may block the oil pump screen, plug small oil lines and passages leading to the valve train, and gum-up piston rings, valve stems, valve lifters.
• At normal operating temperatures the water and the unburned fuel is more completely vaporized and returned to the intake manifold/carburetor through the action of the positive crankcase ventilation system.

OTHER FACTORS AFFECTING
THE COOLING SYSTEM

Efficiency of the cooling system can be upset by any one of the following:
• Late or severely retarded ignition timing may lead to an engine overheating condition and can also cause the exhaust valves to literally "burn-up".
• Since the exhaust system normally removes as much waste heat as the cooling system, anything that reduces the "free-

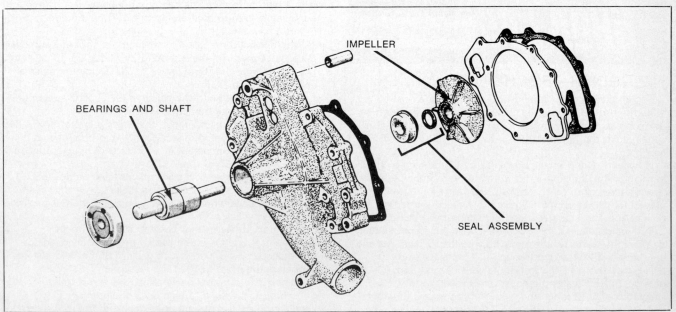

Typical water pump parts. This is an exploded view of a pump installation in a 429 CID Ford-built engine; smaller displacements use basically the same parts.

flow" of exhaust gases (thus increasing back pressure) will result in greater temperatures in the exhaust areas. And if the cooling system is not able to carry away this increased heat load, the results will be a loss of power and early failure of the exhaust valves.

• If the cooling system is operating near its limit and the automatic transmission fluid is running excessively hot because of a low fluid level or poor mechanical adjustments, the end result can lead to an overheated cooling system and transmission problems.

• An air conditioning condenser reduces air flow through the cooling system radiator fins. Also, the condenser gives off heat so that the air reaching the radiator is warmer than one with no air conditioning. It is an important factor to consider when installing one of the "hang-on" types of air conditioners and the reason these manufacturers stress the need for the cooling system to be thoroughly checked during installation.

• Brakes that are "too tight" or "dragging" cause the engine to work harder to reach and maintain a specific road speed, resulting in an overheating condition.

TWENTY STEPS TO A COMPLETE COOLING SYSTEM TUNE-UP

Not all car manufacturers agree on the steps needed to perform a complete cooling system tune-up or the order in which they should be made. However, the following services do cover all of the steps considered the most important when checking out the cooling system.

1. Check the coolant level in the radiator and look for excessive rust or oiliness in the solution. *"Ford's recommendations"* are to drain and refill with fresh permanent type anti-freeze which meets Ford specifications and water mixture every 24 months. Cross flow radiators should have the solution level at the COLD FILL mark. Vertical flow radiators should have the solution level ONE INCH below the bottom of filler neck. When it is necessary to add coolant for any reason (or changing the complete coolant solution), only a high quality inhibited all-season coolant meeting Ford Specifications M97B18-C should be used. The use of alcohol or menthanol type anti-freeze is NOT RECOMMENDED.

WARNING: Use extreme care when removing the radiator cap. Turn the cap slowly to the partially open stop position to relieve internal pressure before removing the cap.

2. Check the radiator cap sealing surfaces located in the radiator filler neck. Look for nicks, deep scratches or damage in this area of the radiator fill opening.

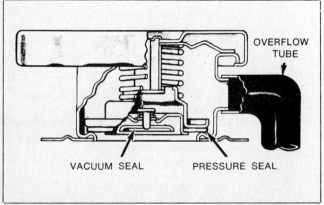

Typical details in cross section of a radiator pressure cap. Note the two sealing surfaces.

3. Check visually for external leaks. Internal leaks and the radiator cap can be tested by a radiator shop with a pressure pump and gauge tester.

4. Pull the engine oil dipstick and check for traces of water or an indication of coolant mixed with the oil.

5. Remove and test the thermostat. Compare partial opening against the factory specifications. With the thermostat removed, place it in boiling water. If it does not open more than ¼ inch, replace it with a new thermostat.

If the problem being investigated is insufficient heat, the thermostat should be checked for leakage. This may be done by holding the thermostat up to a lighted background. Light leakage around the thermostat valve (thermostat at room temperature) indicates that the thermostat is unacceptable and should be replaced. It is possible, on some thermostats, that a slight leakage of light at one or two locations on the perimeter of the valve may be detected. This should be considered normal.

Make sure the heater control valves are operating properly from the full-closed (shut-off) position to the full-open position.

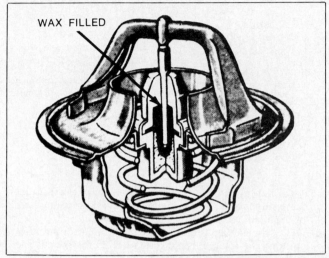

Cross section view of the "pellet" type thermostat installed in Mustangs.

6. Check and test the heat gauge for accuracy.

NOTE: The sending unit (temperature switch) used with the warning indicator light system is NOT INTERCHANGEABLE with the sending unit used with the gauge system. Misuse of the sending units will result in an inoperative temperature indicating system and damaged sending unit or gauges. Perform the test as follows:

7. Start the engine and allow it to run until a thermometer placed in the coolant at the radiator filler cap reads a minimum of 180 degrees F. The gauge in the instrument panel should indicate within the normal band.

If the gauge does not indicate, proceed as follows:

Disconnect the gauge lead from the terminal at the sender unit. Connect the lead of a 12 volt test light or the positive lead of a voltmeter (20 volt scale) to the gauge lead that was disconnected from the sender unit. Connect the other test lead to a suitable ground. With the ignition switch in the ON or ACC position, a flashing light or fluctuating voltage will indicate that the instrument voltage regulator is good and that the gauge circuit is not interrupted.

If a pulsating voltage is shown but the gauge is not accurate, perform a calibration test. Information on this test will be found in your Ford Car Shop Manual.

If the light stays on or the voltage reading is steady, replace the I.V.R. (Instrument Voltage Regulator).

If no voltage is indicated by the voltmeter or test light, check the I.V.R. for proper ground and check for an open circuit in the I.V.R., the gauge windings, or the printed circuit.

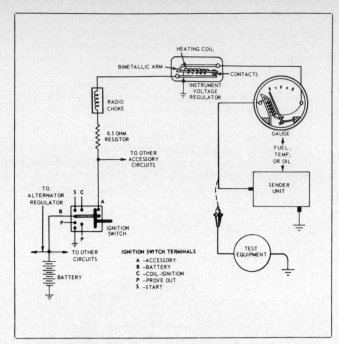

Wiring diagram of the instrument voltage regulator and temperature gauge, 1971 Ford cars.

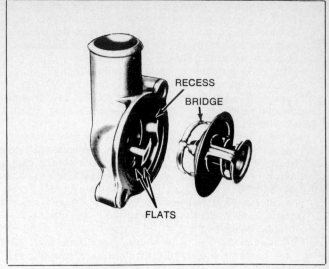

Note the flats and the recess in the housing. The thermostat is properly installed and centered by these surfaces.

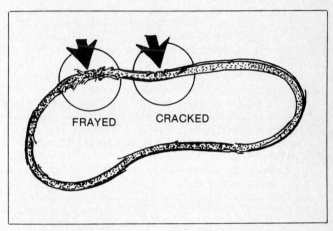

When inspecting any drive belt, look for these two damage conditions and replace if found.

Do not ground or spark either terminal of the instrument voltage regulator. This will burn out the dash wiring harness or the I.V.R. or both.

8. If the coolant is due for a change (24 months use) or you find the solution badly rusted...drain the system and back flush until the water runs clean.

NOTE: The thermostat must always be removed prior to pressure flushing.

A pulsating or reversed direction of flushing water will loosen sediment more quickly than a steady flow in the normal direction of coolant movement in the system. In severe cases where cleaning solvents will not properly clean the cooling system for efficient operation, it will be necessary to use the pressure flushing method. Various types of excellent flushing equipment are available.

9. Clean all leaves, bugs and other foreign objects from the radiator fins.

10. If the outer surfaces of the engine are heavily covered with an insulating "blanket" of dirt, grease, or road mud, then a steam cleaning of the engine should be performed.

NOTE: Avoid steam cleaning near or at the air conditioning condenser in front of the radiator.

11. Remove the fan/water pump drive belt and test the water pump bearings by turning the pulley with your hand. Also check for excessive side or end play. If you find a "rough" bearing or one that has a grating/grinding feel, the pump should be replaced immediately.

12. Rotate the fan and while doing so check the fan blades for alignment and their balance.

If the engine is equipped with a fan-drive clutch, test it as follows:

Spin the fan blade. A resistance to movement should be felt. If there is no resistance, or the opposite... high resistance, you will have to perform a minimum and maximum fan speed test. To do this, see your Ford Car Shop Manual.

13. Inspect the condition of the fan belt and if badly worn, frayed, or cracked, replace the belt.

14. Inspect the condition of the cooling system hoses, the heater hoses, and all clamps. Replace as necessary.

15. Check the cylinder block core hole plugs and the drain cock at the bottom of the radiator for any evidence of leakage.

16. Refill the cooling system with the factory approved coolant and water to bring the protection range down to -20 degrees F. temperature. In climates where temperatures are more severe, you will have to bring the protection range down even further to prevent freeze-up during the winter months.

17. Reinstall fan belt or its replacement and be sure to adjust it to factory specifications.

18. Double check the entire cooling system for any leakage of the fresh solution. Run the engine for at least five minutes to bring engine temperature to normal.

19. Check ignition timing and, if required, reset to factory specifications.

20. If you are servicing a cooling system that has a history of overheating, then check for restrictions in the exhaust system... check for a frozen heat riser valve (if so equipped) and for brake drag. It may be necessary to pull the water pump and check the condition of the impeller blades. Corrosion may have eaten away at the blades and reduced their effectiveness in moving coolant throughout the cooling system.

How To
REMEDY SQUEAKING UPPER CONTROL ARM BUSHINGS

by Donald Farr

You're cool, right? You're driving your gleaming, sparkling Mustang through the local hamburger joint parking lot — not to buy a hamburger, of course, but to show-off your pristine ponycar to the hoards of local hot-shoes who gather ceremoniously every Saturday night. And they're all gazing your way, following every rotation of the styled steel wheels as you prepare to ease over the first speed bump. SQUEAK! SQUEAK! Oh no, not now...! It never fails, just when your ego reaches its highest level, those infamous Mustang upper control arm bushings emit their all-to-familiar shriek of terrifying embarrassment.

What can you do about it? Where does that awful noise come from? The culprits are the 4 bushings that pivot the upper control arms on their shock tower mounting shafts. When these little devils get dry, they squeak. And every Mustang uses the bushings, so the problem is common to all Mustangs, 1964½ through 1973.

Temporarily, you can quiet the bushings by spraying the bushing nuts with penetrant, letting it seep down into the bushings. However, that remedy will cure the squeak for only a short time and soon the noise will reappear. Also, the weather often offers a temporary fix; humid and wet conditions will sometimes silence the bushings, but once the weather turns dry, the squeak will return once again.

The best and most semi-permanent solution is to inject grease into the bushings. That may sound simple enough, and it is for 1965-66 Mustangs — you just remove the bushing plugs, install regular 90 degree grease fittings, and pump in a small amount of grease. However, on 1967-73 Mustangs, the upper control arms fit so snugly inside the shock towers that regular 90 degree fittings won't fit between the control arm and the shock tower wall. We've all seen — all too often — holes cut into shock towers for installing grease fittings. That was the earliest method of getting grease into the bushings, but today there are a couple of better alternatives — and you don't need a torch.

The first alternative comes in kit form from Thexton Manufacturing Company. Thexton's "Trouble Tamer" Upper Control Arm Grease Fitting Kit includes 4 special, 2-piece 90 degree fittings just for the tight-fitting 1967-73 Mustang control arms. There's even a special wrench included for installation.

Installing the fittings is simple enough: raise the front of the car (and support it with jack stands) and remove the front wheels, then remove the bushing plugs, screw in the fitting base, and install the fitting. Nimble fingers will come in handy because of the tight fit. With a hand-pumped grease gun, inject 2 or 3 squirts of grease; don't over do it or you'll pile up excess grease behind the control arm. The Thexton fittings can be left in the bushings, ready for the next squeak fit. Look for the kit at any

15

auto parts store that carries Thexton products, or write Thexton Manufacturing Company, 7685 Parklawn Avenue, P.O. Box 35008, Minneapolis, Minnesota 55435 for the name of their closest distributor. The "Trouble Tamer" kit, part number 560, retails for $12.97.

The second alternative also comes in kit form and is available from your local Snap-On parts distributor. Their Upper Arm Lube Kit (part number GA417)

includes a special wrench for loosening the bushing plug, a unique spinner wrench for removing the plug, and a round lube adapter for injecting the grease. With the Snap-On kit, you replace the plug in each bushing after the greasing. The kit retails for $19.00, but you can reuse it again and again, or even rent it to friends.

One word of warning: the grease will eliminate the squeak but will not cure worn-out upper control arm bushings.

In fact, worn-out bushings will often refuse to take the grease. If you suspect that your bushings are deteriorated, take the car to a reputable shop for inspection and possible replacement. If you've got the tools, you can replace the bushings yourself using the guidelines found in your Mustang's shop manual.

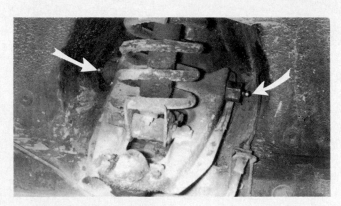

The upper control arms in 1965-66 Mustangs fit into a wide shock tower. Regular 90 degree grease fittings (arrows) are already installed in this 1965 Mustang.

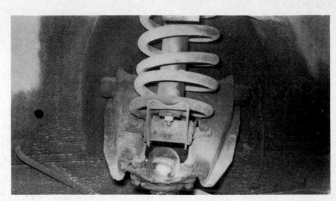

Later model (1967-73) Mustang upper control arms mount in a much narrower shock tower with very little space between the control arm bushings and the tower wall. The grease plug screws into the center of the nut. Disregard the coil spring condition; editor's cars aren't always perfect, you know.

The wider 1965-66 shock towers allow ample room to install regular 90 degree grease fittings...

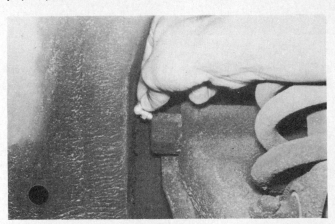

...but the space between the bushing and shock tower wall in 1967-73s is too small.

Snap-On Upper Arm Lube Kit consists of 3 special tools: a plastic "spinner" (left), grease fitting (center), and wrench (right). The bushing plug is shown for reference.

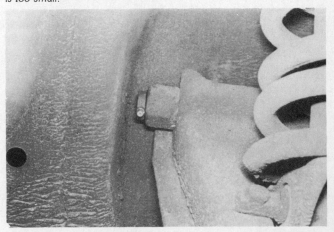

Snap-On's special round grease fitting is a snap (no pun intended) to install. Once the bushing is greased, the fitting is removed and the bushing plug replaced.

16

How To
SELECT CORRECT TIRES FOR YOUR MUSTANG

by Jerry Heasley

We were cruising along I-4 in the Florida sunshine, headed for Tampa International Airport. Larry Dobb's 1966 Mustang GT convertible was wearing radials, knee deep in rubber. "I've always felt that radials tend to 'road-walk' on an early Mustang."

At that time, I wasn't entirely sure what Larry meant by "road-walk", although I had a feeling for what he was saying. But it started an investigation into tires and what type of rubber is best for first generation Mustangs.

Right away we knew that the 1965/1966 models came standard with bias ply tires, and radials were not an option. And we could remember that it was the 1973 model year when the Mustang suspension was first tuned to accept radials. So could it be that the suspension of an early Mustang is incompatible with a modern radial, and that aside from stock considerations, it would be best to shoe a Mustang with bias ply tires (except for the '73's, of course)? What is the difference in radials and bias ply tires then, and the whys and wherefores of using them on early Mustangs? Then too, what about tire sizing? What is the modern equivalent of the 6.95x14 bias ply?

Here's what we found out.

TIRE SIZING

If you've tried to buy new rubber for your Mustang lately, then you know that tire sizing nomenclature has changed drastically since the Mustang was first introduced.

For 1964½ through 1967, and part of 1968, Mustang tires were sized by their "section width" and diameter. Then, beginning with 1968 and through 1973, the "alpha-numeric" system was used. During this change-over period, tire stores used charts to equate the new alpha-numeric system to the older system, which had been in use since about 1925. But if you wanted to buy a 6.95x14 ten years ago, you could usually still find them. Today, this size is obsolete, and a totally new sizing system is coming into use again, known as "P-metric." Ask a tire salesman today what replaces an old 6.95x14, and he'll go to his charts, and eventually confuse himself and you. In fact, the salesman I talked to ended up standing various 14 inch tires alongside the wheel wells on my '66 coupe, looking for a satisfying match with a new "P-metric" radial. My

coupe was already shod with 6.95x14's from Kelsey, and there was no modern equivalent that would satisfy my desire for a stock tire! None!

So let's clear the air and take a look at what the letters and numbers mean in each of the sizing systems mentioned above.

SIZING BY "SECTION WIDTH" AND RIM DIAMETER

For example: 6.95x14

6.95: The "section width" in inches. Section width is defined as the distance from sidewall to sidewall, at the tire's widest point, inflated to the proper pressure, and loaded (on the car).

14: The rim diameter in inches.

SIZING BY THE "ALPHA-NUMERIC" SYSTEM

For example: F78-14

F: The closer this letter to the beginning of the alphabet, the smaller the tire, and the smaller the load rating. If this letter is followed by an "R", then the tire is a radial — such as an FR78-14. At one time, the F78-14 was a replacement for a 7.75x14, and at another date it was a replacement for a 7.50x14. Still, neither replacement was an exact match for the older tire.

78: The "aspect ratio", which is the ratio of the tire's height (distance from the bead to the tread) to the

17

"section width" — the quotient expressed as a percentage. The lower the aspect ratio, the "flatter" the tire. An F70-14, for example, has a lower profile and a wider section width than an F78-14.

14: Rim diameter in inches.

SIZING BY THE "P-METRIC" SYSTEM

For example: P195-75-B-14

P: Stands for passenger tire. A "T" stands for a temporary use spare.

195: The section width in millimeters.

75: The aspect ratio.

B: Denotes bias-ply construction. A "D" stands for diagonal, and also means bias-ply. An "R", of course, stands for radial.

14: Rim diameter in inches. However, some rim diameters are stated in millimeters instead.

Now let's go back to our original question — how to replace a 6.95x14. Converting P-metric sizes to 6.95x14, you will find that no modern replacement tire exactly matches. The P195-75-B-14 is charted as the modern equivalent replacement, but we can easily convert millimeters to inches and see that there are some drastic differences in dimensions here. The aspect ratio of the 6.95x14 is about 83, and the aspect ratio of the P195-75-B-14 is 75. Converting 195 mm to inches (25.4 mm = 1 inch), we have 7.68 inches, which is almost three-quarters of an inch wider than 6.95 inches! A much closer section width, then, would be the 175 mm, which converts to a 6.89 inch figure, quite close to 6.95 — but then the height from the bead to the tread would be 5.17 inches (.75 times 6.89), or considerably smaller than the 5.77 inches of our 6.95x14! That's exactly why the 195 P-metric is the suggested replacement via the charts. Tire height is very important to keep your speedometer reading accurate. With the 195, the height from bead to tread is 5.76 inches, or very close to the 5.77 inches of the 6.95x14 bias-ply — but then the tire is considerably wider than the original! A compromise would be to use the 185 P-metric, in which case both the height and section width would be incorrect, but each dimension would be fairly close, rather than one very close, and one way off the mark.

You can see that before we even talk about original construction, there is no exact tire match according to size — unless, of course, you go to the aftermarket and Kelsey's, which we will discuss later. Also, tire sizes are extremely important for ride and handling characteristics. But have you ever had a radial tire grab the wheel well on your Mustang? So take care when choosing tire sizes for your

Here's a pair of 6.95x14 tires, 1966 above and 1967 to the right, from our factory photograph collection. The 1966 tire is a Goodyear "Power Cushion", and the 1967 version is a Firestone "Deluxe Champion". Ford used both Goodyear and Firestone.

vintage Mustang!

TYPES OF TIRES

Tires are either bias-ply or radial. Bias-ply tires have been around for most of this century, and are so named because the plies are laid down at an angle to the direction of travel. The most common angle, bead to bead, is 45 degrees, which provides a compromise between rolling resistance and rigidity. As you know, most first generation Mustangs came equipped with this type of tire.

Radials were pioneered more than thirty years ago by Michelin, and their plies are laid down at a 90 degree angle to the direction of travel. Therefore, the plies are called "radial." Belts also run the circumference of the tire, helping to eliminate tread distortion and tire squirm. The object is to keep the tire patch in constant contact with the road, rolling straight and true. Any squirm in the tread increases the rolling resistance and builds up heat, which wastes energy and accelerates tire wear. The radial's sidewall is relatively flexible, however, and operates independently of the tread.

An off-shoot of the bias-ply tire, which became very popular in the United States during the late 1960's and early 1970's, was the fiberglass belted bias-ply tire. Most performance Mustangs of that era used some kind of wide oval, belted bias-ply tire. Like the radial, belts are laid down the circumference of the tread, but at an angle to the direction of travel — although at a slightly smaller angle than the supporting plies. As far as friction and gas mileage, this tire is a compromise between bias-ply (with no belts) and radial. The belts have the same function of stabilizing the tire patch, so the belts still serve the tread. But due to both the bias-ply and the bias-belt layout, the plies and belts serve the rigidity of the sidewall, and then the belts also subtract from the rolling resistance of the tire itself, increasing tread life. Notice, however, that we said nothing about out and out performance of the bias-belted tire versus the radial. Have you ever tried a "burn-out" with a radial tire? Once you break traction, it's bye-bye burn-out! Before we leave this subject, it is true that many of today's racing tires are radials, but in truth, the plies are laid down at a very small angle to the direction of rotation, providing some sidewall rigidity. As you know, for a long time radials were more suitable for the street, rather than racing. This situation is changing, but you must remember that there is very little similarity between racing radials on the track, and radials on your street car.

One area where we need more information is radial tire application on certain pre-1973 Mustangs. Despite the charts from the various "Mustang Facts Books", we are in the dark as far as practical knowledge on which cars truly came with these tires, and we want to hear from anybody who can *verify* a Mustang that did come equipped from the factory with radials. Of course, we mean pre-1973, and in particular, the 1968 and 1969 models. Perhaps these tire options were other than for domestic use, and if so, did the car then have some minor suspension differences, or were these radials of a different construction compared to today? Or was the '68 and '69 suspension (standard or GT?) more suited to a radial tire? Are the charts incorrect? Particularly fascinating is the "185-R14(2)" radial tire size in the 1968 "Facts Book." Where did this P-metric size come from in 1968? Was it dubbed-in as a size at a later date? And isn't it interesting that this tire has the 185 millimeter section width that we mentioned at the top of this article, which would best approximate both the section width and the bead to tread height of the 6.95x14?

STOCK OR NON-STOCK?

Anytime you change to a non-stock tire, you technically change your suspension set-up, more or less, depending on the tire. Most drivers tend to overlook this fact, and buy whatever the tire salesman says is the proper replacement. But remember that to the salesman, your vintage Mustang is probably no more than an old car, and he wants to make a sale, which means he doesn't care if you have to compromise. In truth, the right tires are important to the enjoyment of your car, and a vital part of its suspension. You probably would never consider changing the camber, the caster, the spring rates, or the stabilizer bars, because you know that the handling characteristics would change! So give the tires this same consideration!

Tires transmit power to the road, changing the direction of the whole vehicle according to camber attitude and sidewall deflection. So it is both the type and the size of the tire that becomes so important to the vehicle. The tire, in fact, is integral with the suspension, and designed for it.

Now, back to radials on a

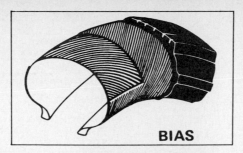

BIAS

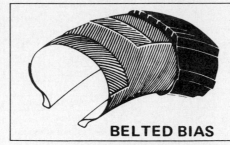

BELTED BIAS

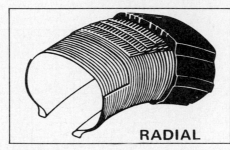

RADIAL

1965/1966 Mustang — or any first generation vehicle that was designed for bias-ply.

Generally speaking, cars built to accept radials have more compliance built into their suspensions. When a radial hits a bump, for example, there is a certain amount of movement that comes out of the tread belt region which is much stiffer for the radial tire. In this case, the rest of the vehicle's suspension has to allow for this added stiffness, which it does. But when the tire is installed on a car such as the Mustang, which was designed for bias-ply tires, this "fore and aft" motion at the tread (which is 90 degrees to the direction of rotation, or longitudinal with the plies) causes a feeling that we might call "road-walk." One engineer at Firestone called it "low speed waddle."

Generally, we can say that radials on a car not designed for radials will exhibit more low speed harshness.

But would a non-stock radial damage the suspension of an early Mustang? Well, common sense tells us that a radial would "work" a suspension more, since the low speed ride feeds back more road imperfections, and is putting more stress on the suspension. Therefore, in the long run, it is possible for a Mustang with radials to wear out its suspension slightly faster.

GETTING THE RIGHT TIRES

Go to any Mustang car show and you will see an assortment of bias-ply,

belted, and radial tires on 1964½-1973 Mustangs.

However, in the last year, the new Kelsey bias-ply "red lines", "dual red lines", and white sidewalls are showing up on Mustangs from California to Carolina. It's good news for Mustangers, because now we do not have to make compromises, and we can again experience the true Mustang ride! If you have been riding on radials or incorrectly sized bias-ply tires, then you are in for a pleasant experience when you change back to stock tires.

I dialed Kelsey's toll free number (1-800-325-0091), and here are the tires they have in stock that you might want for your Mustang:

6.95x14 Red Line, Dual Red Line, White Sidewall
7.50x14 White Sidewall
7.75x14 Red Line
7.75x15 Red Line, White Sidewall

E70-14
F70-14   Red Line
G70-14

F70-15
G70-15   Red Line

The 6.95x14's above are four ply polyester, or practically the same tire as the original two ply rayon construction. It would have been a waste to make the reproduction 6.95x14 in the old rayon, since polyester will give the rayon-type ride with the strength of nylon. You still have the same bias-ply construction, without the disadvantages of rayon. Rayon will take on the shape of the flat pavement if the car is allowed to stand long enough (nylon is even more susceptible). The result is tire "morning sickness", in which you will hear a bump the first few miles of driving after the car has rested in one spot overnight.

Since all Mustang tire sizes, 1964½-1973, are not yet available, we suggest buying as close to the proper size as possible, using the information in this article for sizing. However, in the next few years, we expect to see more discontinued Mustang tires hit the specialty market. Today you can still buy many of the alpha-numeric sized tires, still with the bias-belt construction too, but they are disappearing, and what is sometimes more important is the raised white lettering on the side of the tire is completely wrong as per original specs. But if we support the specialty tire makers, there is little doubt that these tires will soon be reproduced also. If the manufacturer knows that the market is out there, he will make and sell the tires. Perhaps letters to Kelsey Tire, Inc., P.O. Box 564, Camdenton, MO 65020 could get some interest sparked? Then maybe we could see some of those one-inch raised white letter tires again?

1965

STANDARD SUSPENSION					HANDLING PACK	
TIRE SIZE	170 Six	200 Six	260 V-8	289 V-8	260 V-8	289 V-8
6.50x13	Std.	Std.	Std.	Std.		
7.00x13			Opt.*	Opt.*		
6.50x14	Opt.	Opt.	Opt.	Opt.	Std.	Std.
5.60/5.90x15					Opt.	Opt.

*Standard with air conditioning.
  Note: All tires are black sidewall; 13 and 14 inch tires are available in white sidewall.

1966

TIRE SIZE	170 Six	200 Six	289	289 HiPo
6.95x14 Rayon	Std.	Std.	Std.	
6.95x14 Nylon	Opt.	Opt.	Opt.	Opt.*
6.95x14 Premium Nylon			Opt.	Std.

*No-cost option
  Note: 6.95x14 premium nylon tires have dual red-band sidewalls. All other tires are black sidewall with white sidewalls optional.

1967

STANDARD MODELS					GT EQUIPMENT GROUP		
TIRE SIZE	200 Six	289	289 HiPo	390	289	289 HiPo	390
6.95x14	Std.	Std.	Std.				
7.35x14	Opt.	Opt.	Opt.				
F70x14		Opt.	Opt.	Std.	Std.	Std.	Std.

Note: F70x14 tires are white sidewall. All other tires are black sidewall with white sidewall optional.

1968

STANDARD MODELS					GT EQUIPMENT GROUP		
TIRE SIZE	200 Six	289/302	390	427	302	390	427
6.95x14	Std.	Std.					
7.35x14	Opt.	Opt.	Std.				
E70x14*		Opt.	Opt.				
F70x14		Opt.	Opt.		Std.	Std.	Std.
FR70x14		Opt.	Opt.	Std.		Opt.	Opt.
185xR14		Opt.	Opt.			Opt.	Opt.

*Styled steel wheels only
  Note: Wide-oval (E70 and F70) and radial tires are white sidewall. All other tires are black sidewall with white sidewall optional.

1969

STANDARD MODELS								GT
TIRE SIZE	200 Six	250 Six	302	351/390	302/429 Boss	428	428 CJ	Any V-8
C78x14	Std.	Std.	Std.					
E78x14	Opt.	Opt.	Opt.	Std.				
E70x14			Opt.	Opt.		Std.		Std.
F70x14			Opt.	Opt.		Opt.	Man. Opt.	Opt.
FR70x14			Opt.	Opt.		Opt.		Opt.
F60x15					Std.			

1970

Belted Tire Size	Sidewall Color	ENGINE										
		All Models Except Mach 1								Mach 1		
		200 Six	250 Six	302 V8	351 V8	428 Cobra	428 Cobra Jet	302 Boss	429 Boss	351 V8	428 Cobra	428 Cobra Jet
E78x14	BSW	Std.	Std.	Std.	Std.							
E78x14	WSW	Opt.	Opt.	Opt.	Opt.							
E70x14	WSW					Opt.				Std.		
F70x14	WSW			Opt.	Opt.	Opt.	Opt.			Opt.	Std.	
F70x14	B/WL			Opt.	Opt.	Opt.	Opt.			Opt.	Opt.	Opt.
F60x15	B/WL							Std.	Std.			

1971

Belted Tire Size	Sidewall Color	250 Six	ENGINE								
			All Models Except Mach 1					Mach 1			
			302 V8	351 V8	429 CJ	429 CJ-R	351 HO	302 V8	351 V8	429 CJ	429 CJ-R
E78x14	BSW	Std.	Std.	Std.	Std. (a)	Std. (a)					
E70x14	WSW	Opt.	Opt.	Opt.				Std.	Std.		
F70x14	WSW	Opt.	Opt.	Opt.	Opt.	Opt.		Opt.	Opt.	Std.	
E70x14	B/WL	Opt.	Opt.	Opt.	Opt.	Opt.		Opt.	Opt.	Opt.	Std.
F60x15	B/WL		Opt.	Opt.	Opt.	Opt.	Std. (b)	Opt.	Opt.	Opt.	Opt.

(a) F70 WSW required
(b) F60x15 B/WL tires with F78x14 space saver spare

1972

Belted Tire Size	Sidewall Color	ENGINE						
		All Models Except Mach 1				Mach 1		
		250 Six	302 V8	351 2v/4v	351 HO	302 V8	351 2v/4v	351 HO
E78x14	BSW	Std.	Std.	Std.	N/A	N/A	N/A	N/A
E70x14	WSW	Opt.	Opt.	Opt.	N/A	Std.	Std.	N/A
F70x14	WSW	Opt.	Opt.	Opt.	N/A	Opt.	Opt.	N/A
F70x14	B/WL	Opt.	Opt.	Opt.	N/A	Opt.	Opt.	N/A
F60x15	B/WL	N/A	N/A	Opt.	Std.	Opt.	Opt.	Std.

(a) F60x15 B/WL tires with F78x14 space saver spare.

1973

Belted Tire Size	Sidewall Color	ENGINE				
		All Models Except Mach 1			Mach 1	
		250 Six	302 V8	351 2V/4V	302 V8	351 2V/4V
E78x14	BSW	Std.	Std.	Std.	N/A	N/A
E70x14	WSW	Opt.	Opt.	Opt.	Std.	Std.
F70x14	WSW	Opt.	Opt.	Opt.	Opt.	Opt.
F70x14	B/WL	Opt.	Opt.	Opt.	Opt.	Opt.
F78x14	WSW	Opt.	Opt.	Opt.	N/A	N/A
GR78x14	BSW	Opt.	Opt.	Opt.	Opt.	Opt.
GR78x14	WSW	Opt.	Opt.	Opt.	Opt.	Opt.

E70 and F70 — Wide Ovals.

1965-1973 Mustang Tire Availability Specifications

How To
REPAIR LEAKING MUSTANG COWL PANELS

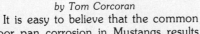

That Cowl Leak Now,
Or Before It Starts...

by Tom Corcoran

It is easy to believe that the common floor pan corrosion in Mustangs results from "up North" road salt. Undoubtedly, some of our rust problems are geograpically related, but we should not forget the vulnerability of these Pony Cars to cowl area leakage. The smallest perforation around the upper vents (the hardest area to reach on a Mustang) can lead to moisture accumulation on the floor pans — often unbeknown to the car owner because, excluding a flood, the carpeting and pads do such a good job of hiding the problem.

Bill DeLoach, in Pensacola, Florida, has an ingenious solution to the leakage problem. He has had to find and test among several products in the hardware stores, and he's had to "invent" some tools to accomplish the job. But when we

compare the results to the efforts, and the cost of these repairs to the potential for underside damage, there is much to be said for this procedure.

First, test actual leaks that can be seen under the dash. You may want to remove the front seats and lay down a cushion for this initial step. However you do it, wedge yourself up under the dash with a flashlight while someone lets a moderate stream of water flow into the middle of the cowl vent grille. The most likely spots for leakage are forward and outboard of the air vent ducts. Whether or not you confirm leakage at this point, you may want to follow the steps below, if only for peace of mind.

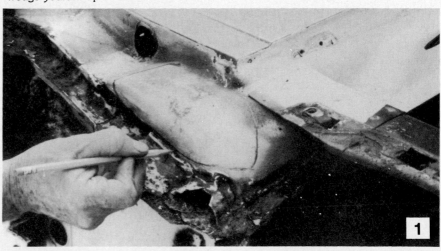

1 - After removing the front fenders, also remove the fender shields which protrude from the unibody just forward of the cowl area. Next, pencil-outline the cut to be made. (On the passenger side, here.)

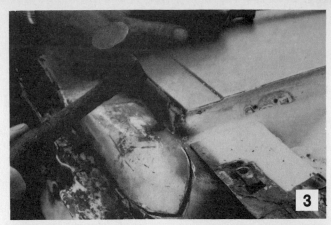

2 - Cutting tool (inset) is fabricated by attaching a small disc blade to a short steel post. This will be held in the chuck of a power drill.
Cut along the scribed line as shown, around the sides and along the bottom of what will become our access hole. Leave the topmost four inches or so uncut. (Note: A sabre saw will not work because the vent air duct is behind the surface to be cut, and will snap the sabre saw blade.)

3 - After cutting all but the top line, tap along this uncut line to start a bend in the metal.

4 - Carefully push the flap upwards to gain access to the inside of the cowl area.

5 - Now, cover the ragged edges of the cut with masking tape. This protects hands and equipment, and leaves the rough-cut edges to grip the body putty when we close the flap.
Reach into the vent duct and pull out accumulated pine needles, mulch, and pieces of rusted metal and dried body sealer.

6 - Another attachment must be made for grinding with the power drill. This is a 36" length of 1/4" steel rod. On one end, cut approximately 1" of 1/4x20 threads, and fit a circular 1¾" coarse wire brush between the two nuts and washers. With this tool, grind anywhere you can see (or suspect) rust.
NOTE: Be sure to close the doors of your heater box to keep trash and paint particles out of the car interior. Use a pressurized air hose to blow out the cowling after various stages of grinding. We recommend cutting into this cowl area on both sides of the car at the same time for an easier and more complete job.
At this point it is a good idea to check out the surrounding exterior area for possible trouble spots. Before we finish this job, we will shoot the entire area with undercoating material, so why not pry away old body sealer. Chances are you will find a few rusty spots which could be future problems. Especially check along body seams where moisture can collect.

7 - One potential trouble spot is a drain which we found (on two cars) dammed by old undercoat. Clean the drain and pry it gently downward so it can drain more effectively.

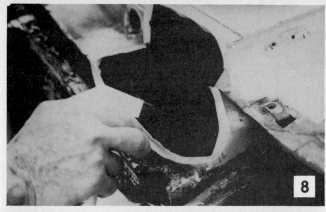

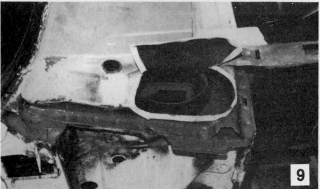

8 - A company called Skyco makes "Ospho". It inhibits and prevents rust; it's a primer, but not a paint. Apply this prep using an old "409" spray bottle instead of a brush. Use plenty and hit all the areas you have taken to bare metal. As Ospho works and dries (for 6 to 8 hours) it darkens the metal.

9 - Finally, it will have a grey, dusty texture.
Next, fill all perforations in the cowl/underdash area with Liquid Metal. Follow this with a coat of Red Zinc-Chromate Primer. To keep the primer off the cowl grille, try spraying through an extension tube from a can of WD-40 or similar aerosol.

10 - Now we go shopping for two 3M products. One is "Body Schutz" (we pronounce it "shoots"), and the other is the Body Schutz Applicator Gun. This is an undercoat-type sealer which hardens shortly after application. (At 70 degrees in moderate humidity, it should take about 15 to 20 minutes.) Mask around the cowl vent grille but don't bother to mask the grille itself. Just be ready to wipe away overspray very quickly as you coat the interior of the cowl area.

11 - Then, shoot around the vent duct and any exterior sections you have prepared in the adjacent area.
If you dare after all this work, test again with the garden hose. Find a leak? Shoot some more of that Body Schutz sealer in there. No leaks? Great.

12 - Push the access flaps downward to close the holes we cut earlier. Fill the cut area with body putty. This, too, can be sealed with Body Schultz.
Sit back and smile. You're ready for final paint, and good for many years of one less headache for a Mustang owner.

MATERIALS:

SKYCO "OSPHO" — 32 fl. oz. plastic bottle, at $5 to $8 depending on your hardware store.

3M "BODY SCHUTZ" — Part No. 08864 — 900 ml. can

3M APPLICATOR GUN — Part No. 8997. Approximately $37. Note: Clean this gun with mineral spirits after use.

How To
BREATHE NEW LIFE INTO MUSTANG AIR CONDITIONERS

by Tom Corcoran with Bill DeLoach
photographs by Tom Corcoran

Eureka, you found it! In a junkyard, in a Falcon! (Or maybe in a Fairlane.) It's an early model hang-on air conditioner system, and it's correct for your model Mustang! Most of the parts are still intact, and hopefully the lines and hoses are hooked up and not exposed to open-air corrosion. Sooner or later it'll get crushed with the rest of the car; you offer to buy its freedom from the yard owner for a twenty dollar bill. He wants a couple twenties. So thirty bucks gets it. It's now your A/C set-up, except it's still attached to the wrecked car.

Remove it with care! There are several reasons for this, and one is for safety.

With an A/C system still hooked up, with all components in place, dismantling should be *slow* and *easy*. First of all, Freon, when released, can cause frostbite. Shield your hands with gloves or rags and eyes with goggles. And second, the system has an array of fragile and easily bent lines and connectors. Why force a kink into an aluminum tube, and add to your expenses? Once you've found your bargain, don't turn it into a monster by breaking or losing parts and brackets.

Also, taking care at this point will tend to control the loss of A/C compressor crankcase oil. Because of the internal pressure at both the top and bottom of the compressor, rapid bleed-down will blow oil out. It will get into the rest of the system, or become a puddle on the ground (or the front of your shirt). Go slowly, and you leave as much of this special oil behind and lose only the pressure charge.

As soon as pressure is out of the system, disconnect the hoses from each unit. Now close off all the openings either with fitted caps (usually available at refrigeration or auto A/C shops), or with tape, to prevent contamination by dirt and moisture.

Check the condition of all the hoses. Severe ozone cracks where you can see the underlying cloth reinforcement dictates replacement.

There are three basic parts of the A/C system. The EVAPORATOR goes under the dash, the CONDENSER is located in front of the radiator, and the COMPRESSOR (which makes things happen) is normally mounted to the engine block. Three other parts will be discussed in the

The three basic air conditioner parts (1965 pictured here, left to right): compressor, evaporator, and condenser.

restoration; the *expansion valve*, mounted atop or alongside the underdash unit; the *filter/dryer* (or receiver), normally attached to the condenser; and the *sight valve* which is fitted into the hose which runs from the dryer to the expansion valve.

The filter/dryer attaches to the condenser. Inside, selica gel crystals absorb any moisture that finds its way into the air conditioning system.

To begin, it is recommended that you replace the filter/dryer if it shows signs of age or contamination. It contains silica gel (or Protosorb) crystals which are a dehydrating agent. With age these crystals break down into a fine dust which can clog your system. In writing this article we found that compressed air blown through the dryer of our junkyard treasure puffed a dirty smoke out of the exhaust hose. That was the broken-down gel, and we had to replace our filter/dryer with a new one.

If your dryer appears to be in good shape, you can reactivate the silica gel crystals by baking the dryer in the oven for about four hours at 150 degrees.

Next, with the hose fittings of the condenser/dryer section recapped, this unit can be washed and cleaned. Light air pressure can be helpful, and light sanding will improve the finish prior to repainting with semi-gloss black. Avoid a heavy paint build-up; this section must transfer heat efficiently. If any coils (or cooling fins) are broken away or loose, they can be reattached with small amounts of good old Bondo as adhesive. Done neatly, it works and saves a welding job.

Now do a final purge of the condenser with Freon-12, and reclose the end caps.

For checking out our compressor, we will jury-rig a belt drive on the workbench. We shifted the drive belt from our vacuum pump to fit snugly enough for the 1/3 HP electric motor to turn the car A/C compressor clutch assembly. (See photo.) Come on now, if you're clever enough to find a Mustang air conditioner in a junkyard Falcon, you're clever enough to rig this thing.

Now, in rotating the A/C compressor, our first test is for

smooth bearing operation when the unit free-wheels. (It always rotates when the engine is running, whether or not the A/C is functioning.) If there is noise in the free-wheel bearings, replacements are fairly easily found. They are held in by snap-rings on each side.

To check the operation of the clutch, we will run two wires from a 12 volt source to the compressor's hot lead, and to ground. You should hear the clutch click when power is applied. Now, with the clutch engaged, rotate the compressor with your electric motor and test with your fingers for both suction and pressure on the external valves. If your fingertips sense the push and pull on the two valves, it's time to hook up gauges to make sure the compressor's doing the work it should. Ideally, it should pull down 29 or 30 inches of vacuum.

Finally, check the crankcase oil of the compressor. This is *not* standard motor oil; it is a special refrigerant oil called Capella, Type "E". In opening your oil servicing port (see photo), don't allow dirt to get inside, and don't lose your brass sealing ring. Oil level measurement will depend on your particular installation. There is a different level for vertical, horizontal, and even 45° mountings. We recommend you check available shop manuals, or with a dealer or repair shop, for the correct level for your system.

The 1965-66 Mustangs use an underdash evaporator unit, while later model Mustangs incorporate the unit within the dash. The 1965 unit pictured here has an argent face; 1966 versions were camera-case black.

Begin work on the underdash evaporator unit by removing the knobs (usually with an Allen wrench), and the 9/16" nuts which hold the fan and thermostat controls. Now, the front of the unit can be lifted off. IMPORTANT! There is a fragile cold-sensing capillary tube running from the thermostat into the evaporator coils: try not to bend this tube! If it breaks, it will become more than just a pesky problem.

To clean the front of the evaporator, remove the Ford medallion and the circular air registers. These registers are held in a track by two tiny flat springs. Use a knife blade to release the springs (and keep an eye on them when they pop out, because they're good for some distance and usually wind up behind shop equipment). *Do Not* wash the chromed plastic air registers with detergent: it removes the chrome. If it's time for new registers, they are available for less than $20 a set from several of our *Mustang Monthly* advertisers.

The front of the evaporator can be cleaned with water and white rubbing compound. The face can be repainted either with Ford Argent for '65 models, or semi-gloss black (Krylon makes a good one) for '66 models.

The main part of the unit should also be washed. Check to make sure the coils aren't loaded up with dirt which has been lifted from the floorboard. Use your 100 lbs. air pressure to clean any accumulation. The housing of the evaporator is fiberglass, and usually in good shape. If needed, it can be repainted with a mixture of near-flat black with a slight amount of brown tint. Refer to a clean original system to verify the color, and the need to repaint.

Next is an electrical check on the evaporator. Again, with wires from a 12 volt source, connect to the hot lead of the fan control switch (on ours, a red wire on the far left side of the switch), and to the ground wire which exits the back side of the unit. Check all three positions. Now, run a 12 volt test

bulb between the ground wire and the compressor clutch lead. Switching the thermostat on and off will test that switch and confirm power to the clutch.

Finally, we get to the expansion valve. It is a very small orifice within the hose connections at the evaporator; it is a variable opening, and is the most likely spot for problems with an old system. Dirt and moisture at this valve can clog the system's operation with crud and ice.

Remove the gummy insulation material from the tubing and connections adjacent to the expansion valve. Depending on your model, all this is located either on the top or the driver's side of the evaporator. New insulation material (see photo) can be obtained from any refrigeration company.

Now, carefully dismantle the expansion valve. Apply air pressure to clear the tiny orifice. It took pressure from both sides to clear our valve. Next, we will blow out the tubing of the evaporator with the compressed air. WARNING. Protect yourself and your clothing from oil spray out of the exhaust tubing with a cloth rag. Having the system oil in there is normal; cleaning it up is a pain in the rear. Continue the air pressure until you are convinced the tubing is clear. Last, purge the unit with Freon-12. Protect your hands with gloves or cloth, and spray the freon through the evaporator. You shouldn't have to directly connect the Freon can if you're careful to avoid frostbite. Now, refit the expansion valve, and cap everything for protection.

In reinstalling the capillary tube at the expansion valve, make sure the bulb at the end of the cap tube is firmly pressed against the tubing when it is clamped down. A false reading from this area will give erroneous info to the thermostat. The air conditioner will attempt to cycle too rapidly, and fight itself for cooling and icing.

Rewrap the valve and tubing with your new insulation material. Make it snug and thorough; moisture on the floormat under an evaporator, if not from a clogged drain hose (which leads through the floorpan, normally on the passenger side), is because the insulation is not effective, and condensation is forming on the exposed tubing.

With everything secure, snug, protected, and looking new, the final steps are the final pump-down and the injection of Freon into the system. Again, the advice of a semi-expert, or guidebook, will help. You may need refrigeration tools to adjust the compressor suction and discharge valves at this point. You must pump down the system to about 30" and continue the vacuum pumping for several hours to properly evacuate moisture.

Then, leaving the negative vacuum on the unit, inject Freon 12 and allow the system to induct as much Freon as it can without the engine running. Then start the car with the system turned on, crack the vacuum hose at the vacuum input valve, and build up until the bubbles in the sight glass disappear. Remember that a bubble or two occasionally coming through the sight valve will give a lower head pressure and adequate cooling. Removing *every* bubble will throw an excess load on the engine.

Now, roll up your windows and roll down the boulevard. Those other cars on the road? They're only jealous, cause we're so cool.

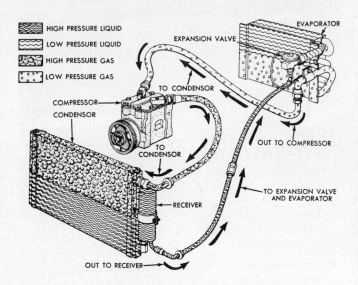

HIGH PRESSURE LIQUID
LOW PRESSURE LIQUID
HIGH PRESSURE GAS
LOW PRESSURE GAS

EVAPORATOR

EXPANSION VALVE

TO CONDENSOR

COMPRESSOR
CONDENSOR

TO CONDENSOR

OUT TO COMPRESSOR

TO EXPANSION VALVE AND EVAPORATOR

RECEIVER

OUT TO RECEIVER

INSTALLATION. Time to bolt it on, run the hoses, align the drive belts, and hook up all connections. We found this chore to be more accurately measured in beers than hours. So stock up.

How To
REFINISH MUSTANG STYLED STEEL WHEELS

by Dr. Dan R. Jones

They are highly sought after as that distinctive finishing touch. They frequently appear on those trophy-winning Mustangs we all envy when the awards are passed out at Mustang shows. They turn heads, even today, especially among non-Mustangers who look at them again and again as you sit out the traffic light. The curious high school kid in his hot rod stares and asks "Where did you buy those...I've never seen them at the Goodyear store..." They are unique. They are beautiful. They are becoming exceedingly harder to find and more costly to own, with one N.O.S. in the box demanding a price at least equal to what the total set originally cost. Even in rough condition, they can be more expensive than today's new after-market mags. What are they? They are "Styled Steel Wheels" — the original Mustang mag.

An early Mustang, particularly high-performance versions, appears incomplete without these wheels. Granted, the wire and spinner wheel covers are beautiful and quite distinctive, adding much to a restoration (not to mention their cost!). But the early '65-'67 styled steel wheels with their unique centers and chrome lug nuts give any Mustang that racy, sporty look which sets off whitewalls or dual red-line tires in outstanding fashion.

Yet, to land a set of these beauties

for your Mustang will require hurtling three major obstacles: locating them, paying the price, and making them presentable. Perhaps my experience in restoring a set for my '65 K-GT may help you overcome some of these obstacles. This article will attempt to describe how to restore '65-'67 styled steel wheels by taking you through the steps used to successfully achieve that end.

LOCATING THEM

This step is a combination of luck (being at the right place at the right time), knowing the characteristics of each year (so you get the right set for your car), and having an awareness of price ranges (so you don't get taken). To begin with, where do you look for a set? The best rule is to search anywhere there are Mustangs and to actually inspect the wheels if possible before buying. This includes the obvious, like Mustang and SAAC shows as well as large swap meets like Hershey, Carlisle, and Raceway. Ads in magazines like Mustang Monthly, Hemmings, etc. will provide information about asking prices as well as making the wheels available to you, but at a trade-off of not seeing the wheels before buying and often paying the shipping cost. N.O.S. wheels may not present a problem, but used wheels, which are what most of us have to start with, can mean uncertainty. This is where the reputability of the seller

comes into play — an unknown seller may mean unknown quality.

Another source is local junk yards, but chances are these have either been cleared out already or the owner recognizes the value of Mustang parts and charges accordingly. I'm afraid that most of us are a few years late in exploring the junkyards as a parts source since most are no longer "undiscovered".

There is also the rare but possible source of the little old lady down the street still driving her Mustang with styled wheels. If she's not interested in selling "Mom's car", pursue her and offer to replace her "old" wheels with new ones (such as standard wheels and covers) as well as paying for the ones on the car. Don't laugh — I know of this having occurred! Finally, there is one additional source...luck. This was my experience, the result of the acute and knowledgable eye of my brother. He sighted a rough '65 fastback on a used car lot in Indianapolis while driving by (in that part of town, one does not stop to browse around the neighborhood). A closer inspection revealed the presence of styled steel wheels, minus centers and correct lug nuts (as is often the case), with four mismatched tires. The Mustang's price was firm — the seller knew he had something because several people had already attempted to buy the car (but not mentioning the wheels). Do not hesitate about the figure for the car (it was not much more than the wheels were worth) since it will cost the chance to buy it. After purchase, the wheels came off, the car was cleaned up and resold with standard wheel replacements.

Another "luck" source is local newspaper and trading magazine ads. Look for unusual descriptions of wheels, such as "Mustang Mags", "Ford Wheels", "GT Mags", etc. These can turn out to be styled steels and may even be priced at an unknowingly low price. Hence, leave no stone unturned in your search.

Knowing the characteristics of each year is crucial for a proper match to your '65-'67 pony. Basically they look very similar but have different trim items. The '65 wheel is a one-piece chrome wheel with no outer trim ring (area is chrome) and has a red center cap. The '66 wheel has chrome spoke area with a detachable outer chrome ring and the same red center cap as the '65. The '67 wheel is similar to the '66 except it has a blue center cap. The wheels should be the same year as the car.

PAYING THE PRICE

How much? That is the key decision. Assuming you have located the wheels and a willing seller, you must make a choice. Do you haggle over price and take the chance that they may be sold when you return to modify your offer, or are you ready to spend the money at the risk of paying too much? Not an easy obstacle to hurtle. Good advice would be to know the current price ranges before searching. A recent review of Mustang-related ads and show vendors revealed that you can expect to pay $50-$75 per wheel in unrestored condition *without* centers (about $13 each), trim ring (about $22 each), or chrome lug nuts (about $2.50 each). This means for a set of five styled wheels you can expect to pay $250-$300+, then you will probably need to buy trim items which can run up to $200 with shipping. Next you need to buy argent styled wheel paint for the "U-shaped" areas between spokes. This is available from many sources advertised in this magazine (as well as trim items) in the $4-$11 range. Finally, the '65 and '66 spare wheel requires a different spare wheel mount plate (part #1424A) and bolt (part #1448D) costing about $5. Wheels already restored can easily top $100 each and N.O.S. wheels have been advertised for $150 each (assume that you will have to add trim items to these). So, you can get into $500 easily even starting with unrestored wheels. With so many styled wheels already on collected Mustangs, supply is becoming a problem. This will make them harder

1965

1966

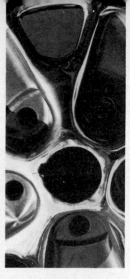

The 1967 styled steel wheel (upper wheel) is ½" wider than the 1966 wheel (lower wheel). Also, the '67's center is slotted for proper alignment of the unique center cap.

Styled Steel Wheel Recognition

Three different styled steel wheels were used on the 1965-67 Mustangs — one for each of the 3 years. All of the wheels feature the same chromed spokes and argent-painted recesses — the differences are found in the rims and the center cap mounting holes.

1965 - The 1965 styled steel wheel is the easiest of the 3 to recognize — the rim is all chrome whereas the '66 and '67 rims are painted black and covered with trim rings. The hub is capped with a red center with an embossed Mustang insignia.

1966 - In 1966, the styled steel wheel was simplified. The rim is painted black and a chrome trim ring used to give the wheel its all-chrome look. The center cap is identical to the one used in 1965.

1967 - With the availability of wider tires for the 1967 Mustang, including the Wide Oval, the styled steel wheel became ½" wider, from 5½" in '65-66 to 6" in '67. The new center cap has a blue center with 5 "fingers" that spread out to meet the wheel spokes. To align the cap with the spokes, the wheel center includes a slot cutout that matches the center cap. In addition, the '67 trim rings are wider than the '66 trim rings due to the wider wheel width.

to find with time and the price will likely continue to rise as a result. Hence, it would be wise to find them *now* in unrestored condition and finish them off yourself. It can be a very satisfying venture.

RESTORATION

Styled steel wheel restoration is fairly easy and requires no special tools. Having never touched a mag before and being one of those guys who messed up every model I assembled as a kid, I discovered a procedure which will allow anyone to create a quality set of wheels in six steps (with tires removed). These wheels were '65s but the procedure will work for '66 and '67 wheels also. It is assumed that you are starting with wheels which are not damaged or missing excessive chrome from wear. The condition of the chrome, amount of rust, and degree of bent outer rim (common drawbacks to unrestored condition) should not only influence how much to pay but will determine how well the restoration procedure will work. If the rim area is

seriously bent or the wheel has serious rust and missing chrome, you must first straighten the rim and consider what to do about the chrome. Keep in mind that properly rechromed styled steels must be split apart, rechromed, then welded back together — a job for a professional only, or you could end up with out-of-balance wheels and/or burnt chrome from the welding. This decision should also be kept in mind at the time of purchase (again, knowledge before hand is essential to a successful venture).

The six steps for restoration are:
1. Cleaning
2. Stripping Paint
3. Chrome Preparation
4. Taping-Off Wheel
5. Painting
6. Mounting & Installing Trim

STEP 1: CLEANING — Unrestored wheels have old, if not incorrect, paint in the recessed areas between each spoke - along with rust, dirt, and grease. All of this should be removed, beginning with dirt and grease. Wash the wheel thoroughly on both sides. Next, use a cleaner (e.g., Ditzler DITZ-O Wax & Grease Remover, DX-440) on the chrome side and clean the entire surface. Use 000 steel wool to avoid scratching yet permit removal of grease. Be careful when scrubbing rusty areas so you do not remove chrome along with dirt. If steel wool does not remove the rust, then carefully attempt to remove it with a soft wire brush (rotor type) on a hand drill. The surface will scratch somewhat and will show through new paint and unpainted chrome. You'll have to judge how much possible damage you can tolerate in exchange for rust removal. Much of the rust will occur around the holes in the wheel and scratches here are less noticable when the lug nuts are in place.

STEP 2: STRIPPING PAINT — The old paint must be removed. Again, with very fine steel wool, clean the U-shaped areas with lacquer thinner and frequently wipe clean. This may require a series of scrubbings until all paint is gone and shiny chrome is revealed. After the paint is removed, clean the area again as in step 1. (Word of caution: once areas are painted, do not clean any area of wheel with lacquer thinner.)

STEP 3: CHROME PREPARATION — Next, the unpainted chrome area of the wheel should be further cleaned and polished — *before* painting - with a good quality chrome product. Do not polish the areas to be painted.

STEP 4: TAPING WHEEL — The five recessed areas between the spokes must be isolated by taping. This is a very time-consuming process and requires both practice and patience. Use 2" masking tape in strips along the bottom and sides of the U-shaped area. Then lay a piece across the top (nearest hole) and two lower corners so they lay *beyond* the edge of the recessed area and protrude into the painted portion. Press all tape down firmly and carve the exact edge desired along the curves and corners of the U-shaped area. Following the contour of the edge, cut the desired outline with a razor knife, removing excess tape as you go. Be sure no gaps exist along the taped edge. When completed, only the chrome area which should have paint will be exposed. Complete the taping/cutting process one recess at a time. Finally, cover any remaining exposed chrome on the wheel with tape. Newspaper can be taped around the rim and folded back so that, when finished, everything on the wheel is covered except the five U-shaped recessed areas between

The Mustang Monthly "guinea pig" - a well worn, used, and abused 1965 styled steel wheel.

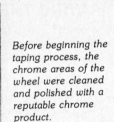

After cleaning the wheel thoroughly, the old, incorrect paint inside the recesses was removed with lacquer thinner and fine steel wool.

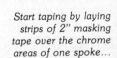

Before beginning the taping process, the chrome areas of the wheel were cleaned and polished with a reputable chrome product.

Start taping by laying strips of 2" masking tape over the chrome areas of one spoke...

...then, very carefully, use a razor to trim the exact shape of the recessed area. This step will require some practice. If you don't get it right, peel off the tape and start again.

When all of the recesses are taped off, cover the rim of the wheel with newspaper. Secure with masking tape.

With the taping completed, only the recesses areas to receive paint will show.

Apply the paint with thin coats to prevent runs. Be sure to cover all areas of the recesses. Leave the wheel stationary while you move around it.

Allow the paint to dry for 24 hours, then carefully remove the tape to reveal the fruits of your labor.

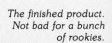

The finished product. Not bad for a bunch of rookies.

spokes. I would recommend that you complete one wheel through Step 5 before doing more since you will improve with practice and correct errors on subsequent wheels after completing your first. If you are dissatisfied with the first wheel, repeat steps 2, 3, and 4 before painting again. Time carefully spent with taping will have the greatest impact on the finished wheel's appearance, so take your time.

STEP 5: PAINTING — Use one of the styled steel wheel paints available from Mustang supply ads. Argent is the proper color. Two 13 oz. cans will easily do 5 wheels. No primer is needed. Paint in warm, dry weather - outside if possible. Follow paint can instructions. Apply the paint in thin coats (perhaps a dozen will be needed), making contact with the different portions of the recessed area (sides, bottom, etc.) with each coat. Avoid applying it too thick, especially to the sides, to prevent runs. Be patient and allow coats to set-up before adding more paint. I found that placing the wheels on a picnic table and walking around the table in repeated passes to work best. You do the moving and leave the wheels stationary. After all coats are applied, let the paint dry 24 hours. When removing the tape after drying, great care is needed to prevent peeling paint off with the tape. Remove the tape in sections, pulling off in a straight, lifting motion. The painted areas should not be polished or buffed hard for a month.

STEP 6: MOUNTING AND INSTALLING TRIM — The mounting of tires onto your newly refurbished wheels can be nerve-racking and potentially destructive to the finished product. Shop around for a tire dealer who will be willing to exercise due care in the mounting process. Often, the kid operating the mounting machine is a car buff and, with a $5 tip, will exert extra care (well worth the money). Be sure the chrome side of the wheel is covered with something to protect it when using their tools. Have the wheel balanced.

Once the tire is mounted, the center cap must be installed before the wheel goes on the car. Next, place the wheels on the car and install the chrome lug nuts carefully. They should be covered with a piece of cloth under the lug wrench socket. Tighten by hand rather than an air wrench to avoid scratching. On '66 and '67 wheels, install the trim ring by popping them into place by hand or rubber mallet. It would be wise not to trust these installation steps to someone else, for lack of care can damage $150 worth of trim items.

There you have it. A set of wheels which will not only increase the beauty of your car but also boost your ego since their "re-creation" was a result of your effort.

SHIFTER FIX!

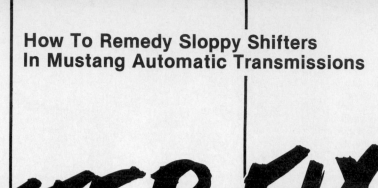

by Donald Farr

Yck! There's nothing in this Mustang world more irritating than a sloppy automatic shifter — it's like shaking hands with a loose-gripped man. I'd rather tolerate a clicking lifter or a whistling carburetor than a rattly, floppy shifter handle. It can make a $10,000 Mustang seem like a $600 junker. You can't even put it out of your mind; turning up the radio will camouflage that noisy lifter, but you can't even back out of the driveway without touching the shifter. Luckily, the solution can be found down at your friendly Ford dealer's parts counter. All you'll need are 2 Transmission Console Shift Selector Shaft Bushings, part number D5ZZ-7A133-A. They're simple to install, and, best of all cheap.

The tools needed for the job can be found in most tool boxes: a Phillips screwdriver, needle-nose pliers (standard pliers will suffice), ratchet, extension, 1/2" and 5/8" sockets, and a 7/64" Allen wrench. Even the most fumble-fingered Mustanger should be able to perform the replacement within an hour, unless the car is equipped with a console which must be removed for access to the shifter housing.

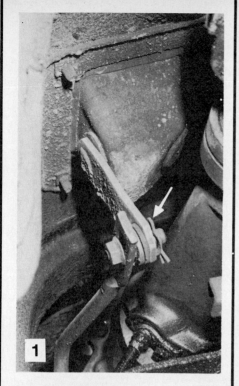

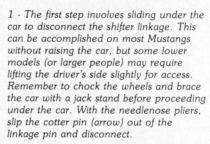

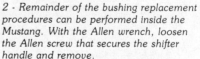

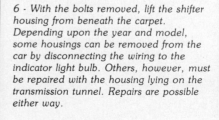

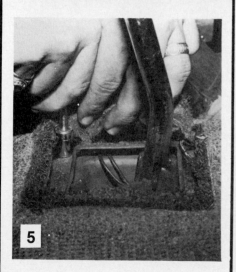

1 - The first step involves sliding under the car to disconnect the shifter linkage. This can be accomplished on most Mustangs without raising the car, but some lower models (or larger people) may require lifting the driver's side slightly for access. Remember to chock the wheels and brace the car with a jack stand before proceeding under the car. With the needlenose pliers, slip the cotter pin (arrow) out of the linkage pin and disconnect.

2 - Remainder of the bushing replacement procedures can be performed inside the Mustang. With the Allen wrench, loosen the Allen screw that secures the shifter handle and remove.

3 - Remove the 4 screws that attach the shifter indicator bezel to the transmission tunnel.

4 - An additional plate must be removed from early Mustangs.

5 - The shifter housing is secured by 4 bolts hidden under the carpet. In some cases, the carpet must be slit at the corners to gain access to the bolt heads. Don't worry; the shifter indicator plate will cover the tears. Use a ½" socket and ratchet to remove the bolts.

6 - With the bolts removed, lift the shifter housing from beneath the carpet. Depending upon the year and model, some housings can be removed from the car by disconnecting the wiring to the indicator light bulb. Others, however, must be repaired with the housing lying on the transmission tunnel. Repairs are possible either way.

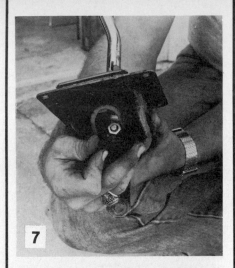

7

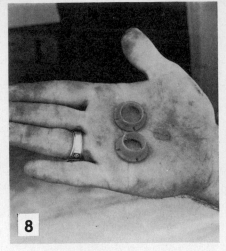

8

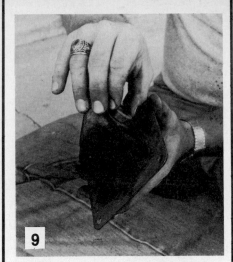

9

10

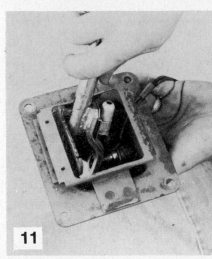

11

7 - With a standard screwdriver, carefully pry off the rubber plug on the shifter housing side to reveal the shifter handle mounting nut. Using a 5/8" socket and extension, remove the nut and separate the shifter handle from the exterior linkage shaft. The remnants of the old bushings, if any are left at all, will be between the housing and the linkage shaft.

8 - The actual bushings are just small plastic pieces.

9 - Slip the new bushings into the linkage shaft hole, one on the outside of the housing and the other on the inside.

10 - Ease the linkage shaft through the bushings, making sure the inner bushing stays firmly in place.

11 - Reassemble the shifter handle, tighten the nut, and replace the rubber plug. Then reinstall the shifter housing into the car in the reverse order of its removal. Remember to reattach the shifter linkage under the car, double-checking the cotter pin for tightness (it may need replacing).

While you're at it...

The automatic shifter selector seal is usually good for only a few years before tearing apart, revealing the inner workings of the shifter and allowing foreign particles to fall into the shifter housing. With the shifter bezel removed for the bushing replacement, it's a good time to replace that worn seal. Simply slip the old seal off the pair of small pins and insert the new seal. Your shifter will look better, and perform better for a longer period of time.

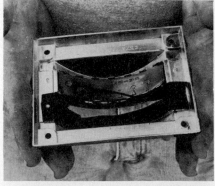

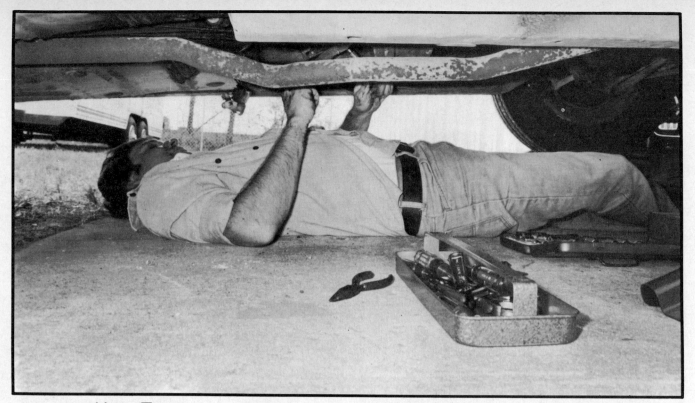

How To
ELIMINATE SHIFTER RATTLE IN MUSTANG STANDARD TRANSMISSIONS

Getting the Shake, Rattle, and Roll Out of 1965-68 Mustang 3-speed and 4-speed Shifters.

by Donald Farr

If you own a 1965 through 1968 Mustang with a manual transmission, then you probably know the sound. It starts in first gear as a slight buzz, and the vibration of the shifter handle in your hand tells you the sound is coming from deep within the shifter mechanism. Second gear, and the sound worsens, becoming more of a rattle than irritating buzz. By third gear, you're ready to yank the shifter from its moorings and sling it out the window.

Fortunately, all you need are 2 shifter handle grommets (379998-S), 2 springs (C2AZ-7208-A), and 2 retainer caps (C2AZ-7B125-A). Best of all, the parts fit both the 3 and 4-speed shifters and list for less than 6 dollars.

Getting to the manual shifter's inner workings is a little more difficult than an

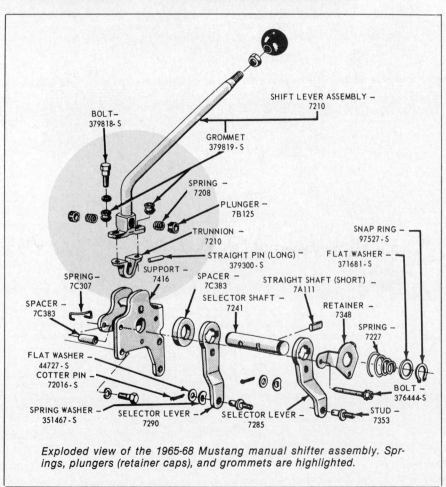

Exploded view of the 1965-68 Mustang manual shifter assembly. Springs, plungers (retainer caps), and grommets are highlighted.

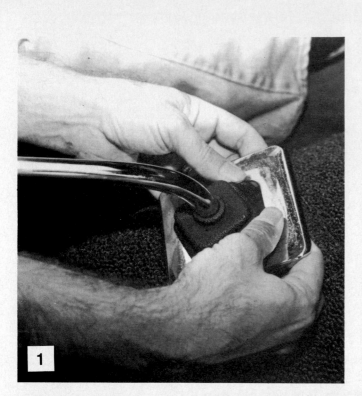

1 - It's much simpler to replace the shifter grommets and springs from the car's interior, however, you may have to cut or remove the carpet to get the rubber boot out. With the boot removed, the shifter can be repaired from the top without removing the unit from the car.

2 - The second alternative requires a little more effort. First, raise the front of the car to gain access underneath. We used drive-on ramps, but a jack and stands will work just as well. Above all, make sure the car is supported safely and the wheels chocked to prevent rolling. The shifter is mounted on the left side of the transmission tailshaft, secured by bolts and covered by a dust boot. The heavy black wire connects the back-up light switch.

3 - First, disconnect the shifter linkage by removing the cotter pins and sliding the linkage aside. Then unbolt the back-up light switch and wiring, letting it hang out of the way.

automatic (see Shifter Fix in the December '81 issue), but any average backyard mechanic can perform the task in less than 2 hours. The shifter mechanism can be exposed 2 ways: from the car's interior or from underneath. From inside the car, you'll have to remove the chrome boot trim (or console, if equipped) and the rubber boot, which may require front carpet removal. The boot's base is made of hard rubber and will not slip through the hole in the carpet. If the carpet is old, you can slit the corners enough to get the boot out — the slits will be covered by the chrome trim later. The grommets and springs can then be replaced without removing the shifter unit.

In our case, we elected to remove the shifter from the Mustang, mostly because we didn't want to remove or cut the new carpet in Howard's '66 hardtop. The procedure was simple enough — disconnect the shifter linkage and unbolt the shifter housing from the transmission tailshaft — until we tried to maneuver the unit away from transmission. A mounting plate on the tailshaft limited the shifter movement and had to be removed. Simple enough, we thought, until we discovered the large Phillips-head screw that held the plate in place. A trip to the local tool store produced the correct tool, and the shifter practically fell out with the plate's removal. Later, we learned that the mounting plate is found only on 1966 Mustang 6 cylinders with the 3-speed transmission. Just our luck.

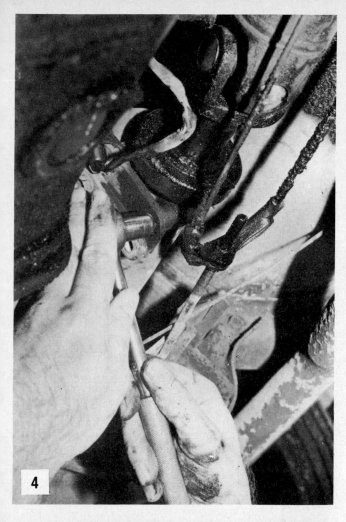

4 - Three bolts fasten the shifter unit to the tailshaft.

5 - Here's the plate and Phillips-head screw that created our grief. A local tool supplier furnished the socket tool needed. Luckily, these plates are found on 1966 six cylinders with 3-speeds only.

6 - Three-speed (left) and four-speed shifter mechanisms are very similar. Repair grommets, springs, and retainer caps fit both.

7 - Two special bolts attach the shifter handle to the shifter mechanism. Springs and retainer caps (arrow) allow sideways movement.

8 - Remove the 2 bolts and separate the handle from the shifter unit.

9 - Repair kit consists of 2 grommets, 2 springs, and 2 retainer caps, all the pieces needed to quiet a noisy manual shifter from 1965-68. Shifter style changed in 1969.

10 - The springs and retainer caps fit into holes on each side of the shifter handle. In many cases, a grease build-up within the holes must be cleaned out, but leave enough to lubricate the retainer caps.

11 - Rubber grommets fit into the shifter handle base...

12 - ...and the shifter handle attaching bolts pass right through.

13 - Tighten the bolts securely and check the shifter movement. Then reinstall the shifter and reconnect the linkage.

Getting the "rag" out of ragtops.

How To
REPLACE YOUR MUSTANG'S CONVERTIBLE TOP

by Art Mullins

Few jolts can compare with the shock of a cold trickle of water dripping down the neck, unless it's the asking price of the average early sixties Mustang convertible. A new top will do more for your pet pony car than keep water off you — it'll keep water and the resulting rust away from the floor pans.

Replacing a convertible top is possible for the home restorer. Most of the advertisers in Mustang Monthly have replacement Mustang tops available at a reasonable price. In the Washington, D.C. area repro tops go for about $95.00. Installation is extra if bought from a Mustang supply house and your game plan calls for the installation by a professional trimmer.

A convertible top replacement is not an easy job or one that should be undertaken by a person who has no trim or upholstery experience or someone who has not piled up a gang of hours as a shadetree mechanic. And the job requires tools; among them: chalk or crayons, phillips and plain screwdrivers, hammer, staple gun, spray adhesive, assorted wrenches and sockets, tape measure or yardstick, and masking tape. And patience.

The top on the '68 Mustang shown in the photos had begun the inevitable shrinking at about four years of age and the rear window was about as transparent as a 289 manifold. Putting the top down on a cold day finally shattered the rear plastic window. The convertible is the property of your correspondent's wife who guards it jealously. A new top and window would earn a passel of badly needed brownie points, lost when yours truly was discovered removing four shiny wheel covers from her dishwasher. Just to make sure, a glass window instead of the plastic would be installed with the new top.

News of the Seatco, Inc. new line of Mustang replacement items had reached me and a quick chat with affable managers, Neal Ailstock and Tim Grinnings, set up an appointment for the ragtop transplant. Frank Padgett, trimmer par excellance, is to auto trim what Frank Sinatra is to music, and agreed to do the job.

Frank believes that careful removal of the old top is an important step of installing the new one, a fact based on 35 years experience in auto trimming and the replacement of about ten thousand tops.

Start with the top down, and remove the rubber weatherstrip from the side rails, the windshield header assembly and the tension or retainer cables. Now raise the top and clamp the No. 1 bow to the header. (Bows are counted one through four from the windshield back.) Take out the No. 2 and No. 3 bow listing retainers and screws. Raise the top and remove the well screws and bolts from the tacking strips. Remove the No. 4 bow outside molding and end tips molding and molding retainer. Now take everything loose from the No. 4 bow and peel back the top material. Next, mark the back stay padding location at the No. 4 bow and tacking strip (down in the well). Mark the No. 4 bow at both ends of the elastic material and remove upper half of the zipper unit from the No. 4 bow.

If you haven't guessed by now, the bottom line is to mark everything in relationship to the attaching points and the new top, using the old one as a guide. It would be helpful to remember that the job consists of three units: new top assembly, back curtain-window portion and the well-compartment unit. From the center mark on the belt center

1 - First things first, Seatco trimmer Frank Padgett covers the deck lid with foam rubber to protect the finish. He then strips off the old top, taking care to leave the side pads in place.

2 - Frank uses an air tool to remove the old tacking strips from the front bow. Notice the top is folded back.

3 - Frank uses a rotary air tool to grind off oxidation from the front bow. This portion has been covered by fabric, the oxidation can be seen as lumps. Uncovered it looks like white powder. This part of the front bow is aluminum.

4 - Part of Frank's exacting standards includes the application of primer to the sanded and brushed front bow to prevent a reoccurence of oxidation.

5 - Using a time-saving air riveter, the old master rivets in a new tacking strip on the front bow.

6 - After the front bow would stand inspection in an operating room, Frank sprays on adhesive before recovering the bow with a new pad.

retaining strip, transfer the mark to the (old) rear curtain and compartment trim items. Now do the same for both sides of the rear window opening and bottom of the corner deck quarters. At this stage you've almost got the old top out — now carefully remove the old material from the tacking strips. Once you have it out on the table, mark all the old attaching holes and points on the new top.

This is a good time to examine the top pads running along both sides of the top from the first to the fourth bow. Managers Ailstock and Grinnings explain that it's better to recover the old pads with new, heavy vinyl top material than to use the available replacement pads, which don't seem to hold up. The old pads were removed one at a time for recovering. They were removed singly to avoid changing the bow location. The old rear window was in place during this operation.

One thing guaranteed to give auto trimmers a galloping case of the surlies is to show up for a new top with the old one completely removed. This has been done a number of times because finicky Mustang owners do it to repaint the bows.

Now it's installation time. Place the new top over the framework, adjust and center the top in position. Raise the top and insert a spacer between the front bow and

windshield. Remove bolts from the rear tacking strip to release curtain from the car. Lift out the rear curtain assembly from the rear of the car. With all the attaching markings on the new assembly, line up and attach to belt center tacking strips. Frank prefers to remove the belt tacking strips from the car and attach the window assembly on the bench. Line up the belt side front tacking strip with the aligning marks and attach both sides of the top deck quarter with staples. Do the same with the top back stay webbing.

Place the upper half of the zipper unit on the No. 4 bow, lining up the center marks on the material and the bow itself with the upper edge of the material flush with the front edge of No. 4 bow. Staple from the center out. Now, position the rear curtain and fasten the zipper, then staple the top of the back stay webbing on the alignment marks of the No. 4 bow. A good idea now is to mark the underside of the top material at the center of No. 4. (Many prefer to use masking tape and mark it.) Mark the centerline along the entire length of the tape. Attach the belt center and side front tacking strip attaching screws to about one-half inch from right. Now center the top on No. 4 bow and pull it forward enough to center the outside bonding seam to No. 4 bow. Staple the top to the No. 4 bow.

Nearing the homestretch, install the two retainers in the No.

2 and No. 3 bow listings. They're the thin metal strips that slide in the fabric strips attached to the underside of the top. They fasten with screws from the underside.

Insert the quarterdeck retaining cables through the hold-down sleeves in the top material and loosely retain each cable at the rear with its nut and washer. Pull the top trim material forward over the No. 1 bow until the listings from No. 2 and No. 3 bow listings are centered over their respective bows. Keeping the material tight, place a pencil mark on the outer surface of the trim material along the front edge of the No. 1 header bow. Fold the front edge of the top material back from No. 1 bow. Loosen the No. 1 bow from the windshield header and prop it up a few inches above the header. Lower the No. 1 bow onto the header but do not clamp it. With the top material centered at the No. 1 bow, start at the outer front corners and pull the material forward to the pencil aligning mark. Remove all wrinkles and fold and cement the material to the underside of the bow. Seal and staple the windshield header and trim off excess top material. Cement the front and rear flap to each side rail. Punch holes in the flaps for the rubber weatherstripping screws.

Install the front side rail weatherstrip and the No. 1 bow retainer. Now tighten the retainer cable nut at each rear side rail enough to hold the top material tightly against the rail, and install the middle and side rail weatherstrips.

Frank warns against some of the aftermarket replacement weatherstripping. In his opinion it's not very good — the fit is bad and the durability is poor.

With the No. 1 bow clamped to the header, tighten all belt tacking strip attaching screws. Install the well compartment trim. Remove the centerline tape strips and install the No. 4 bow outside molding retainer, then insert the molding and the two end tips. That should complete the job except for clean-up.

Time for the job? About four and a half hours.

About the brownie points from the missus. Things were going great until she found some freshly painted plastic seat trim in the microwave oven.

Back to the drawing board.

A stubborn rivet protrudes too much for Frank's liking so out it comes and another goes in. Replacement pad fabric lies on the front bow.

Frank removes the side pads taking care to do it one at a time so the bows do not lose alignments.

CARING FOR FINICKY FASTENERS

The zipper has come a long way since it's introduction at a world's fair before the turn of the century, but the best zipper in the world requires a certain amount of care — especially your convertible's rear window zipper.

The zipper should be kept clean and dry. The zipper should also receive lubrication in the form of a good quality wax at least once a season — more if the climate is hot and damp.

Third, and more important, most zipper problems occur when the convertible owner puts the top down during the heat of the day and zips up when the temperature cools. To avoid trouble caused by the shrinkage of vinyl plastic, keep the top partially up until the back window is completely zipped up. The strain is equally distributed throughout the zipper.

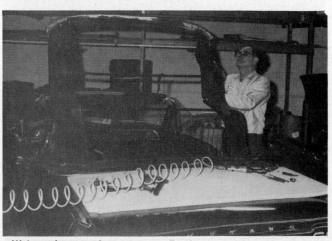

With top frame in the up position Frank removes the side pad and other hardware.

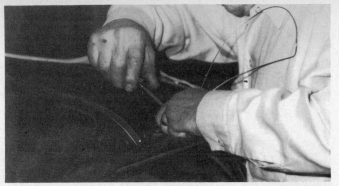

The side tension cables are removed by pulling forward through the retaining sleeves.

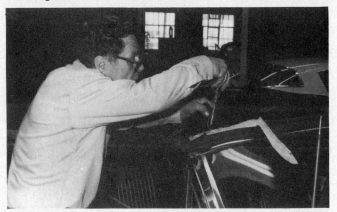

Rejuvenated side pad is reinstalled by Frank from the front of the car. Original pad was recovered with new fabric.

The action changes to the bench. Here Frank attaches the rear window to body bow. Folding glass window was chosen over the plastic.

Frank pulls the top back curtain window assembly to center the rear window.

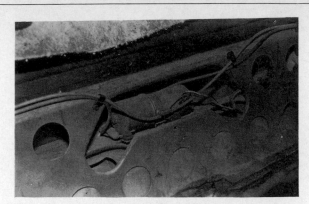

UPS AND DOWNS OF THE POWER TOP UNIT

There's no denying the ease and convenience of a power top on your Mustang convertible. A flick of the finger can really cause heads to turn in admiration, but a sluggish power mechanism can cause you to look all wet — in more ways than one. Listed below are some of the more common complaints and remedies.

PROBLEM - Motor runs but top motion is weak or doesn't move at all.

SOLUTION - Check for low fluid level. The cylinder should be filled with Ford automatic transmission fluid to one-quarter inch below the filler plug opening. The fluid reservoir must be vented before filling, which is quite simple, just remove the filler plug. To gain access to the motor and reservoir, open the top to a fully raised position. Open the deck lid and cover the luggage compartment floor in case of oil spills. Access can also be gained by removing the rear seat back support.

PROBLEM - Top moves in one direction only.

SOLUTION - Check dash switch and wiring from switch to motor. Also check for bad power cylinder or binding of the cylinder rods. Check for binding in the top linkage.

PROBLEM - Top does not retract or rise from the well.

SOLUTION - Check the top control switch, battery charge, circuit breaker; air in the hydraulic system or insufficient hydraulic fluid.

PROBLEM - Top action is sluggish.

SOLUTION - Check battery, motor and pump, wiring, hydraulic cylinders, or air in the system.

PROBLEM - Top does not stack properly.

SOLUTION - Check the balance link bracket adjustment.

PROBLEM - Side rails do not fit.

SOLUTION - Door window adjustment, toggle clamp adjustment, center side rail adjustment, and the top should not be raised with the windows up.

PROBLEM - Top does not latch.

SOLUTION - Top was lowered when wet causing fabric to shrink or it could be a toggle clamp adjustment.

PROBLEM - Top leaks.

SOLUTION - Toggle clamp adjustment, door window adjustment, quarter window adjustment or check weatherstripping.

The rear body bar has been reinstalled in the car and the rear window is attached. Here Frank pulls the top to the upper bow to center it.

New top in place. Frank pulls the top forward to tighten it up and center it.

Frank marks the top lightly with chalk for an adjustment.

Before tightening up the side and center tacking strips, Frank pulls the top taut to remove wrinkles.

RAINING INSIDE YOUR CAR?

When moisture collects on the ceiling of your convertible, relax, it's not leaking, it's condensation. The moisture collects on the ceiling of your car for the same reason it collects on the side of a cold drink or your windshield — or your bathroom mirror.

Condensation is a natural phenomenon, occurring when moisture-laden warm air collides with a cold surface. The air cools off and drops some of its moisture on the nearest surface.

At home you cope with the situation by opening a window, allowing faster circulation of air, and by equalizing temperatures. For your auto windshield you turn on the defrost blower or open the windows. Fortunately, the convertible top does not collect as much moisture as the windshield, because it's not as dense and can't get as cold.

To avoid excessive moisture in the car, which can trigger a host of problems, check to make sure your doors and windows are leak-proof, that your trunk is watertight, and rain doesn't enter your car in any way.

But condensation isn't all bad. That's the principle of physics that makes your air conditioning work.

CARE OF THE
REAR PLASTIC WINDOW
Or Through A Glass Darkly

One of the most widespread complaints of the rear plastic window is its tendency to scratch and fog. To avoid scratching, wash the window with plenty of water and a mild detergent. Do not wipe off when there is dust or dirt on the surface.

To avoid fogging or drying of the plastic, try to keep the plastic window out of the sun as much as possible. The plastic actually sunburns just like your skin, a preservative coating will filter out some of the harmful rays and soften the plastic. A number of plastic window treatments are on the market. One of the best is available from a large auto mail order house, and improves visibility dramatically. It doesn't last long in the rain, however.

Do not clean the window with abrasive preparations such as Comet, Bon Ami, or pumice stone solutions. Avoid the use of strong chemicals such as petroleum derivitives and lacquer thinners.

These recommendations come from a large plastic manufacturer.

How To
CONVERT 1964½-65 MUSTANG IDIOT LIGHTS TO GAUGES

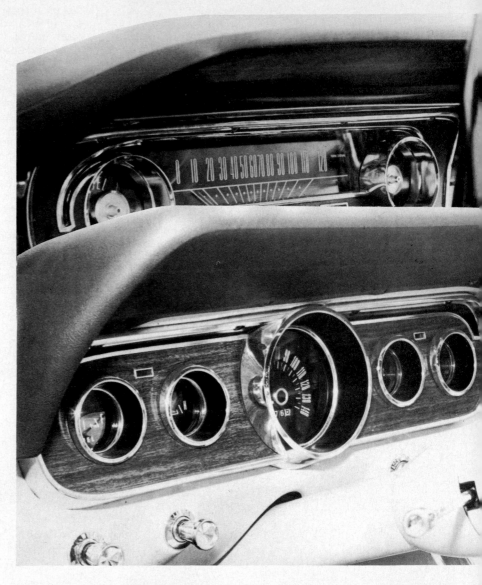

by Sam Ridgeway

In 1965, the new-style 5-dial instrument cluster was found only on Mustangs equipped with either the GT Equipment Group or the Interior Decor Group. Standard model 1965 Mustangs received the Falcon-style speedometer with round fuel and temperature gauges, but the oil pressure and ammeter functions were relegated to warning lights. For 1966, all Mustangs were updated to include the 5-dial instrumentation.

Many of today's Mustangers, especially those adding the GT and/or Interior Decor options to their cars, wish to update their 1965 Mustang with the 5-dial cluster. The simplest conversion is to obtain the instrument cluster (and glove box door — the bezels must match) from a 1966 model and install them in the '65. However, authenticity will be sacrificed because the chrome trim on the '65 GT cluster and glove box door differs from the '66 (see Instrument Cluster Recognition side bar).

Once you've found the correct cluster for your Mustang, you can begin the installation. But what about the wiring hook-up? It is different — if you try to simply transfer wires from the original

'65 cluster to the 5-dial set-up, the gauges will not work properly and only one turn signal will function. The following instructions should get your 5-dial cluster performing correctly.

While you're at the junkyard removing the 5-dial cluster, pick up a used oil pressure sending unit (the oil pressure gauge requires a different one) and extension fitting. If you're converting a V-8 model, make sure the sending unit comes from a V-8. These items are still available new from Ford.

Here's a list of materials you'll need before beginning:

1. 10' of 16 ga. red wire.
2. 10' of 16 ga. yellow wire.
3. Several feet of any other color 16 ga. wire.
4. An assortment of wire splice lugs.
5. A good assortment of crimp-on wire terminal ends or lugs, including 3/16" and 3/8".

6. Two single wire sockets with bulbs, for the turn signals. (Be sure these fit the openings in the rear of the new instrument cluster.)
7. Oil gauge sender and extension fitting.
8. Four #10-32 nuts.
9. Wiring tape.

INSTALLATION

1. Disconnect negative battery terminal.
2. Remove steering wheel. (Not absolutely necessary but it will make the installation much easier.)
3. Tape several layers of newspaper around the steering column to prevent scratching.
4. Remove turn signal lever. (This is just to get it out of the way.)
5. Remove speedometer cable from speedometer head.

6. Remove cluster screws and pry cluster down with your fingers from the top with outward pressure.

7. With cluster hanging loose draw a sketch showing the various colors of wire to their respective hook ups.

8. Disconnect all wires and light sockets and remove the cluster.

AMMETER WIRING

A. At Starter Relay.

1. Remove main power (black with yellow stripe) from forward stud of starter relay. This is the wire with a lug containing both the black wire with yellow stripe and a smaller diameter plain yellow wire.

2. Cut the smaller diameter yellow wire lug off, strip 1/4" and crimp on a new lug to fit the starter relay forward stud. Open up the wire loom tape enough to put the yellow wire on the forward stud of the starter relay.

3. Crimp a lug large enough to fit the forward lug of the starter relay onto your new piece of red wire and install it on relay stud.

4. Leave the main power wire (black with yellow stripe) from which the smaller yellow wire was cut off the forward stud of the starter relay. Install all other removed wires from the forward relay stud and tighten nut.

B. At Alternator (or generator)

1. Remove adjustment lock screw and belt, rotate the alternator and prop it up with a piece of wood to make connections accessible.

2. Remove alternator output lug nut (black with yellow stripe wire) from alternator or generator large stud. Temporarily remove the output wire.

3. Loosen or remove tape from wire bundle extending from alternator to starter relay.

4. Re-route the main power wire (black with yellow stripe from which the smaller diameter yellow wire was cut at the lug) so that the main power wire will reach the alternator or generator output stud. Install this wire on the alternator stud.

5. Crimp a lug large enough to fit the alternator large stud onto your new yellow wire and place it on the large alternator stud. Replace original alternator output wire (black with yellow stripe).

6. Replace and tighten alternator large stud nut. Re-tape wire bundle as necessary. Replace and tighten belt.

C. At Firewall

1. Twist the new yellow and red wires around one another and feed them through the various wire holders toward the fire wall along the route of the brown and red/blue stripe starter relay control wires.

2. If possible, feed the new red and yellow wires through a hole in the fire wall to reach the instrument cluster. If

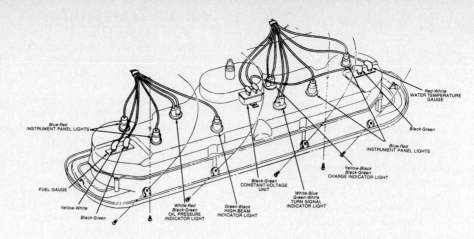

1965 instrument cluster wiring.

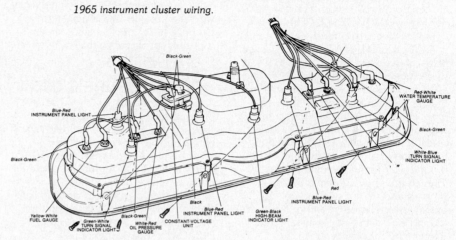

1966 instrument cluster wiring.

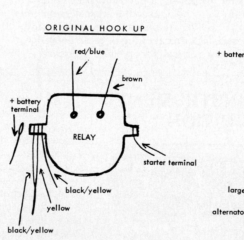

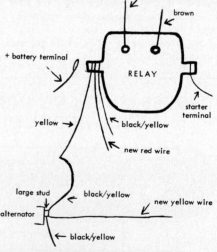

no hole is accessable or large enough, drill a hole large enough to run the wires through the fire wall. Use a rubber grommet or tape the wires so they don't chafe on the metal.

OIL PRESSURE GAUGE WIRING

A. At Left Front of Engine

1. Disconnect the wire from the pressure sensor switch unit.

2. Remove the pressure sensor unit.

3. Install the extension fitting and oil pressure gauge sending unit. Position the extension so that the sending unit

connector stud is positioned up and a little toward the back.

4. Remove the female slide connector from the wire and crimp on a 3/16" lug and connect it to the sending unit.

INSTRUMENT CLUSTER CONNECTIONS

1. On the back side of the new instrument cluster, mounted just to the left of the speedometer, is a devide called a Constant Voltage Unit (CVU). Transfer the CVU to the opposite side of the speedometer in the same relative

position. Drill a hole and attach it with a sheet metal screw. It must be attached secure and the screw must be long enough to be loosened and have a wire attached to it later.

2. Position the new instrument cluster face down on the steering column with the top of the speedometer toward you.

3. Looking down from the top of the cluster connect the new red ammeter wire to the left stud of the ammeter and the new yellow wire to the right stud. The new wires should be shortened appropriately and have lugs crimped on them. Attach the wires to the lugs with #10-32 nuts. This completes the wiring for the ammeter.

4. The Constant Voltage Unit has two black/green wires that connect to it with matching connector slide-on studs. The CVU and cluster must be grounded to the car frame. Cut a length of 16 ga. wire, about 8 to 12 inches and crimp a lug onto each end. Remove the sheet metal screw that attaches the CVU to the cluster and connect one end of the ground wire to the mounting screw. Tighten the screw. Route the wire forward and, at the steering column brace, attach the other end of the ground wire with a sheet metal screw. (Note: You may have gotten the ground wire with the new instrument cluster (black wire) but this is difficult because it is incorporated into the wiring loom and has to be cut off or removed when removing the cluster).

5. Connect the two black with green stripe wires to the CVU.

WATER TEMPERATURE GAUGE

1. Connect the push-on connector of the Constant Voltage Unit output wire (black with green stripe) which connects to the female slide connector of the CVU, to the left hand terminal (looking down) of the water temperature gauge. Connect the original red/white temperature gauge wire to the right terminal.

FUEL GAUGE

1. Locate the original fuel gauge yellow/white wire and connect it to the right hand terminal (looking down) of the fuel gauge. Locate the other black/green constant voltage unit in-put wire and connect it to the left terminal. Do not use the original black/green wire that connected to the left terminal of the fuel gauge.

OIL PRESSURE GAUGE

1. Locate the original two wire oil pressure signal light socket wire (black/green and white/red) and cut off both wires. Crimp a lug on the white/red wire and install it on the right hand terminal (looking down) of the oil pressure gauge. Tape the end of the other original oil pressure warning light wire (black/green) and tape it to the wire bundle for permanent stowage.

2. Cut a short length of new 16 ga. wire and crimp a lug on one end. Install the lug on the left terminal (looking down) of the oil pressure gauge.

3. Locate the original black/green wire that attached to the left hand terminal of the original fuel gauge. Splice (with a three wire splice

connector or other method) the other end of the new wire which is attached to the left terminal of the oil pressure gauge to the original black/green fuel gauge wire.

TURN SIGNAL LIGHTS

1. Locate the original two wire (green/white and white/blue) turn signal indicator light socket and cut both wires from the socket.

2. Splice on a single wire socket with bulb to each wire allowing enough length to reach the new positions using the green/white wire for the left turn signal and the white/blue wire for the right turn signal. Do not try to use the original turn signal socket and bulb.

MISCELLANEOUS

1. Locate the original charge indicator light socket, remove the bulb, tape over the end and tape it to the wire bundle for permanent stowage.

2. Install all instrument panel light sockets into cluster. All panel lights have blue/red wires except high beam indicator which is green/black.

3. Reconnect negative battery terminal. Turn on lights and check panel lights and high beam indicator light.

4. Start engine and check all gauges for proper function, radio, heater, turn signals, etc.

5. Stop engine and disconnect negative battery terminal.

6. Carefully, push instrument cluster into opening making sure all wires are free and light sockets stay in place.

7. Install cluster attaching screws and connect speedometer cable.

8. Reconnect battery.

1965-66 MUSTANG INSTRUMENT BEZEL RECOGNITION

Four different bezels were used on the 1965-66 Mustang instrument clusters. The first, of course, utilized the old Falcon-style instruments with warning lights and a horizontal speedometer. Later in 1965, when the GT Equipment Group and Decor Interior became available in March, models equipped with those options received the new 5-dial instrument cluster with gauges instead of the earlier warning lights. As you can see from the illustrations below, the '65-style 5-dial panel contained a half-circle concentric outline trim ring along the top of the panel. Interior Decor models were covered with a walnut applique while standard interior GT models received a camera-case black finish.

In 1966, standard interior Mustangs were equipped with a similar camera-case black instrument bezel, however, the concentric ring encircles the whole bezel outline. Interior Decor bezels are identical to the ones used in '65, including both the walnut applique and half concentric outline trim ring.

1965 standard instrument bezel.

1965-66 with Decor Interior (walnut applique).

1965 standard interior with GT Equipment Group.

1966 standard interior.

How To
READ MUSTANG ELECTRICAL SCHEMATICS

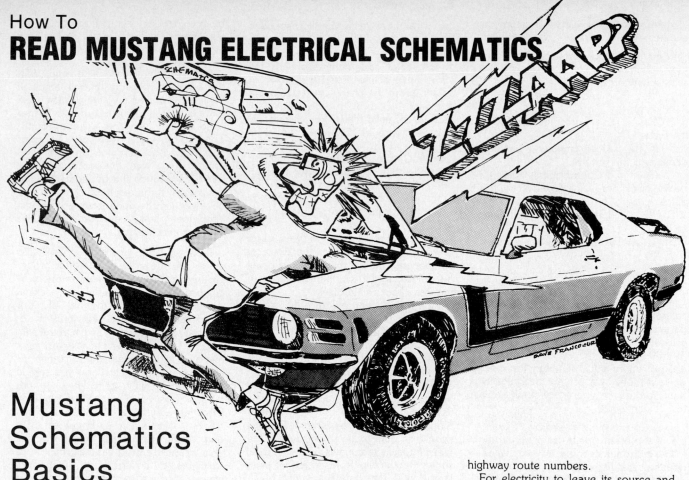

Mustang Schematics Basics

by J.R. Gillespie

By the time we purchase our Mustang, there have been numerous modifications to them, especially to the electrical systems. Wires have been cut and spliced to add stereos, speakers, tachometers, and lights. During major accident repairs, it was always easier to cut and splice wires rather than replace them. In time, many of these splices corrode due to poor insulation, causing short circuits, open circuits, and other electrical system failures. In most instances, the splice is no more than two wires twisted together covered with a piece of tape, if that much.

With a basic wiring schematic and D.C. test lamp or volt meter, you can trouble shoot and repair many electrical failures yourself. D.C. test lamps can be purchased for about $6.00 from most major department stores, automotive parts stores, or electronic shops. Volt meters are available at most electronic shops, but they are expensive for the limited use they would receive from the average backyard mechanic.

Electrical trouble shooting procedures could fill an entire detailed book. Here we will present only a basic introduction into reading schematics and how to trace a simple circuit on your car.

Electrical failures, like mechanical failures, should be diagnosed. Anyone can replace a fuse or a light bulb; but what caused the fuse to fail or bulb to burn out? Will the problem reoccur?

You, as the electrician, should determine what caused the failure. You should also determine which systems are functioning correctly and which are not.

To the average backyard mechanic a wiring schematic - or wiring harness assembly - looks like a puzzle that would take an electrical engineer to figure out. But it's not really so complicated once you become acquainted with basic schematic and electrical symbols.

Schematics and pictorial diagrams for 1965-68 Mustangs can be found in your shop manual electrical section. Manuals after 1968 do not contain complete schematics. Wiring diagram manuals (schematics) for most years can be ordered from many of the Mustang parts advertisers for about $3.00 to $6.00 each.

Schematics illustrate all electrical components, switches, wires, connections, and battery. They also include graphic illustrations and labels for each major component: numbered lines leading from one component to another, and a wire color code chart.

Think of reading a schematic as reading a road map. A road map shows routes that connect one place to another and, similarly, a schematic shows wire routes. The lines represent actual wires identified by wire numbers much like highway route numbers.

For electricity to leave its source and travel to the using electrical component, then return to the source is known as a circuit. The electricity has completed a round trip. Your house uses two separate wires - one to bring electricity in, and the other to carry it out. This is called a two wire circuit. Automobile electrical systems do not have a wire to carry electricity back to its source. Most automobiles utilize a single wire circuit, using the metal parts of the car as the return wire. Most circuits use the body, engine, or frame as a ground return. Whenever you see a symbol like this ⏚ on a schematic, you've located the ground or return. Every circuit must have at least one ground.

A good GROUND is just about the most important part of any circuit. Without it, your electrical system will not function properly. Remember, the ground is the return wire and requires good connections. Paint, corrosion, grease, and oil make for poor ground connection and trouble.

OPEN CIRCUITS are breaks in the hot wire preventing electricity from traveling from the battery to the using electrical component and then back to the ground.

SHORT CIRCUITS generally happen in two ways; the first would be the grounded circuit: a hot wire going directly to the ground causing the fuse or circuit breaker, if there is one, to blow. The second type occurs when the hot wire insulation wears through two or more wires, and touching bare wires cause electricity to detour from one electrical system to another - with some very strange results.

There are various symbols reflected on most schematics which normally are not self explanatory:

1. ⏚ Ground - acts as a return to the battery.

2. ⊶⊷ Fuse - prevents damage to the system.

3. ⊶⊷ Circuit Breaker - prevents damage to the system.

4. ⏺ Common Point or Splice - a heavy black dot, wires connect at this point.

5. ⊗ Male Connector - elements stick out.

6. ○ Female Connector - holes.

7. ⇥ These wires are not connected, they are drawn this way for convenience.

A 12 volt automobile electrical system cannot physically hurt you. The secondary side of the ignition (spark plug wires) will get your attention quickly with up to 30,000 volts, but the very low amperage will not injure you, although the quick upward movement of your head against the hood may leave a nasty bump and a few choice words.

Let's trouble shoot a very simple example of the license plate lamp circuit and follow it through its route. Say you've determined that both the bulb and fuse are okay, but let's assume the lamp will not illuminate when the lights are turned on.

On the schematic, locate the graphic illustration for the license plate lamp. Trace the wire (line) from the license plate lamp; you'll find the wire number is "14B". In one corner of the schematic, a "wiring color code" chart converts the wire numbers into actual wire color or colors. From the chart, you'll determine that wire 14B, 57A, 57, 38, 14C, 14A and 14 are solid black. For all practical purposes, wire 14, 14A, 14B, and 14C are one and the same wire or wire assembly. On the wire color code chart you will notice that most wires have two colors. The first color is always the base color of the wire, while the second color is the stripe which runs the entire length of the wire.

The pictorial diagram in your shop manual, if one exists, for the electrical component you are trying to locate will make locating that component and wire harness a much easier task.

Return to the car and trace the license plate lamp wire into the trunk. Inside, again locate the wire by its color, but it soon disappears into a bundle of wires sheathed in black tape. How do you trace the wire now? Once again consult your schematic. You'll need to find the route between two points by tracing the wire by its number along its path to the point of termination. From the schematic, you should be able to determine where the wire physically terminates. The schematic shows that the wire from the license plate lamp "14B", right hand rear lamp "14C", and left hand rear lamp "14A" terminates at the light switch wire "14". At the light switch, once again find the correct wire by its color code. With the lights on, your test lamp or volt meter will determine if you have 12 volts at the light switch.

Return to the license plate lamp. With the lights on, observe the tail lamps. If they are working and the license plate lamp is not, you can assume the license plate lamp housing has a poor ground. This can be verified with your test lamp: attach one lead (alligator clip) to a good ground and, with the probe from the other lead, touch the hot contact inside the socket. If the test lamp lights up you have verified the poor ground. If the test lamp does not light up, you can assume an open circuit exists.

If the tail lamps and license plate lamp fail to light up after checking for proper grounding, you can look for an open circuit between the light switch and sockets. At this point, with the aid of your schematic and manual, you must systematically trace wire "14" back to the light switch. Make voltage checks with your test lamp at each connector as you go. At some point along the route, you should find a broken wire, corroded plug contacts, or even a disconnected plug. By following a systematic method of circuit tracing, voltage checks using a test lamp and visual inspections, you should be able to analyze most basic electrical malfunctions and correct them. When more serious electrical problems are apparent which you cannot solve, take your car to a qualified automotive electrical repair shop for analysis.

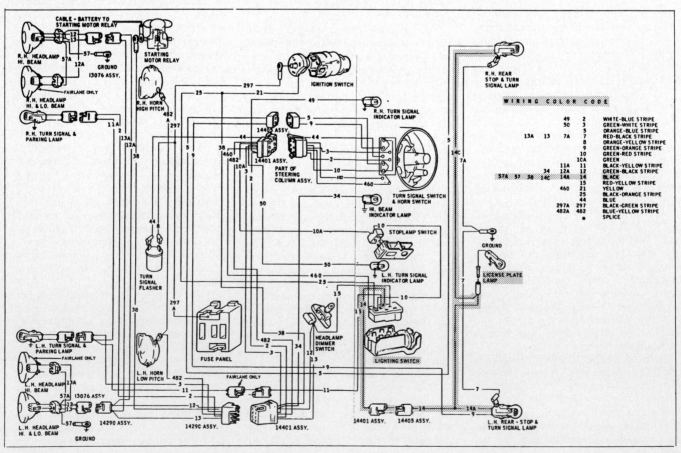

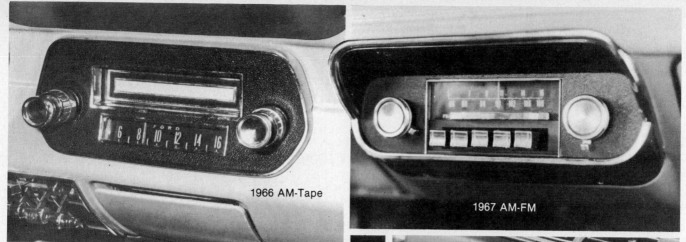

1966 AM-Tape

1967 AM-FM

1966 AM-FM

1967 AM-Tape

How To
FIND AND IDENTIFY MUSTANG RADIOS

by Craig Rickard

During the Mustang years, Ford Motor Company offered several different types of sound systems as optional equipment in the 1964½-73 Mustang. Included were a bevy of AM radios, AM/FM monaural, AM/FM stereo, and AM/8-Tracks. Identification and application can be a problem for today's Mustangers without prior knowledge of part numbers or available systems for the particular year Mustang at hand. The following is a compilation of information acquired over the years as a result of my interest in Mustang sound systems.

Mustang radio identification can be broken down into two categories: visual and part number. The photographs included in this article will assist with visual recognition. With respect to part numbers, Ford used 2 different types. The 1964½-1968 radios received a 4 to 5 figure number stamped on the side casing (i.e. 5TPZ, F7TBZ). These numbers indicate the unit's precise application. For instance, with the number F7TBZ, I can obtain the following: a) 7 stands for 1967, b) B stands for Bendix (M-Motorola, P-Philco), c) Z stands for Mustang as it does in the standard Ford part number. I am still unsure of the significance of

the other digits, but as you can see I have already identified the radio as a 1967 Mustang radio made by Bendix.

The second type of part number found on the 1969 and newer radios is the standard-type Ford part number (i.e. C9ZA 19A242 B). The prefix alone identifies this latter radio as a 1969 Mustang unit. As a general rule, if either type part number contains the last digit of your model year and a 'Z', you can be pretty sure the radio was made for your car.

Now you should be able to look at a swap meet radio and determine its specific 1964½-1973 application. By the way, as far as I know, radios from 1964½ Mustangs contain the number '5' in the part number and not '4'. Many times the question is asked "Will this radio fit in my car?" This is where interchange information comes in handy. The Hollander Interchange Manual, commonly known as the wrecking yard bible, lists several interchanges for the early Mustang radios. My manual covers through 1972 and states that an AM radio from a 1964-65 Falcon will fit a 1964½-1966 Mustang. Also listed is the interchange between 1969-1972 Cougar and 1969-1972 Mustang. This is the only interchange information provided, but

with a little visual inspection and a couple of measurements, I found that there is indeed more interchange. For example, a 1967 Cougar AM 8-track will fit in a 1967 Mustang that originally came with an AM radio. It's a bolt-in operation with no cutting required. The dial might say Mercury but the 8-track will still fit the car. This is only one example of many other interchanges. As far as I know, there is complete interchangeability within each year between AM, AM/FM, and AM/8-tracks. One notable exception is the 1966 AM/8-track which requires enlargement of the existing AM radio opening for installation. When in question about an interchange, simply use a ruler to measure the width, depth, height, and length of volume and tuning shafts with respect to the face.

Bench testing a radio is really quite easy. There are usually 2-3 connectors emerging from the radio (assuming that the leads haven't been cut). Two-connector radios have the speaker terminals on one connector and the dial light and power on the other. Three-

TOP - 66 AM Radio (6TPZ, Photofact #AR 36). 1965 model is not shown but case is larger and dial starts with 6 (not 5). Interchangeable with 1966. Part number 5TPZ (Philco) or 5TMZ (Motorola). Photofact #AR 28.

BOTTOM - 66 AM 8-Track less faceplate (T6SMZ, Photofact #AR 35). Not shown is the 66 AM-FM which has same size face as AM, chrome slide bar with "Ford" on front, chrome push buttons (F6TPZ, Photofact #AR 39). Excellent pictures in Mustang Does It and Mustang Recognition Guide.

TOP - 67 Cougar AM radio (7TPG).
BOTTOM - 67 Cougar AM 8-Track (T7SMW). Included to show similarity between Mustang radios of same year. These interchange with Mustang.

TOP - 67 AM Radio (7TPZ, Photofact #AR 41). Note chrome push-buttons.
BOTTOM - 67 AM 8-Track (T7SMZ, Photofact #AR 45). No push-buttons. The 67 AM-FM (F7TBZ, Photofact #AR 46) is shown on page 22. Notice the similar appearance to the AM radio but with chrome slide bar with no wording. The 67 AM-FM is not stereo.

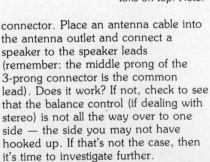

TOP - 68 Mustang AM (8TPZ. Photofact #AR 48). Note Philco name on dial and black plastic push buttons.
MIDDLE - 69 Mustang AM-FM radio (F9BZ or C9ZA 19A241 A, Photofact #AR 64). Same style as 1968 with indicator light for stereo and "stereo" on slide bar.
BOTTOM - 68 AM 8-Track (T8MZ, Photofact #AR 51). Note push-buttons on top. Note: These 3 basic styles were carried on into the 70's.

connector radios (66 Mustang AM for example) have the speaker terminals also on one connector, the dial light on one connector, and the power lead on one connector. Monaural radios have a 2-prong speaker connector while stereo radios are 3-prong (left-common-right). The center lead on the 3-prong connector is the common lead for both left and right speakers. All 8-tracks are stereo and therefore have 3-prong connectors while the first AM/FM stereo was not offered until 1968. Earlier models are 2-prong monaural. Bench testing is easy with a 12-volt power supply. Negative from the power supply goes to the chassis ground while positive goes to the power-light

connector. Place an antenna cable into the antenna outlet and connect a speaker to the speaker leads (remember: the middle prong of the 3-prong connector is the common lead). Does it work? If not, check to see that the balance control (if dealing with stereo) is not all the way over to one side — the side you may not have hooked up. If that's not the case, then it's time to investigate further.

What if the connectors are cut off? The following deciphered wiring color codes should be useful:

Power — usually black for 65-66 radios; yellow/black stripe for later radios.

Dial Light — blue or blue/red stripe.

Speakers — a) 2-prong monaural, black plus black/green stripe, b) 3-prong stereo, white and orange for speakers (left & right), purple in the middle as common lead.

Be careful: an incorrect hook-up may damage the radio electrically. An old wiring harness or a parts radio can come in very handy for splicing good connectors onto the cut wires so that the radio, prior to dash installation, may be plugged directly into the underdash wiring. To do this, first slip some heat shrinkable insulation over the cut wires and slide up over the area to be soldered. After skinning, splicing, and soldering, slip the insulation over the bare connection and shrink with a

TOP - 69 AM 8-Track (C9ZA 19A242 B, Photofact #AR 66).
MIDDLE - 70 AM 8-Track (D0ZA 19A242 A, Photofact #AR 86). Word 'Mustang' is found on tape door.
BOTTOM - 71 AM 8-Track (D1ZA 19A242, Photofact #AR 104). Note similarity between years and presence of 2-prong connector (power and dial light) and 3-prong connector (speakers).

This is my parts radio (below). Not from a Mustang but full of interchangeable parts to aid in repairing Mustang radios. A very worthwhile investment.

This is a copy of Sam's Photofact reference (AR 45 to be exact). If you need an electrical schematic for a 1967 Mustang AM 8-Track, this is where to look.

cigarette lighter or heat gun. It makes for a very nice connection with less chance of shorting. Speaking of parts radios, it pays to buy a couple of junk radios or 8-tracks (Mustang or not) to be used strictly for parts, i.e. push buttons, connectors, tape heads, motors, transistors, etc. I've been using an early 70's Fairlane AM/8-track to repair my 68-73 Mustang AM/8-tracks. That's the best $3 I've ever spent.

This article has by no means covered all there is to know about Mustang sound systems, so the following is a list of references that I have found to be very useful:

1) Mustang Does It by Ray Miller
2) Mustang Recognition Guide by the Editors of Mustang Monthly
3) Yearly Ford Shop Manual (lists part numbers)
4) Sam's Photofact Reference

The later is a very useful reference for the do-it-yourselfer. It contains the

electrical schematics necessary for repair. To use this book, obtain a Photofact Annual Index which is published yearly and is available in most electronics stores. Using the index, look up the radio part number and it will tell you what issue of Sam's Photofact contains the needed schematic. If the electronics store does not carry the desired back issue, some main libraries carry it and it can be borrowed for making photocopies.

RALLY "PAC"

RALLY PAC FEVER

How To
REPAIR AND INSTALL MUSTANG RALLY-PACS

by Donald Farr

There seems to be something prestigious about a Rally-Pac straddling an early Mustang's steering column. Indeed, if you check the current going prices for used Rally-Pacs, you'll be forced to believe in their prestige. In spite of inflated figures ranging to and beyond the $300 mark, the Rally-Pac clock and tach continues to be a much sought after Mustang accessory.

Although the supply of Rally-Pacs cannot be considered abundant, Mustangers are still blessed with enough to go around...usually. Six different versions were produced from 1964½ to 1966, each one designed

for a specific engine and instrument panel (warning lights versus gauges). So while a Mustanger can generally locate a good used, or even an occasional NOS, Rally-Pac, finding one for his or her specific application can sometimes become frustrating.

APPLICATION AND IDENTIFICATION

For initial identification purposes, Rally-Pacs fall into 2 basic styles: hooded (sometimes called 1965) and low-profile (often called 1966). The 2 units are easily distinguished; the hooded version has a hood, like a ball cap bill, over each lens and most have the words "Rally-Pac" spelled out

Rally-Pacs were produced in two very different styles during 1965-66: hooded version (left) has a large web connecting the tach and clock; low-profile style (right) is webless.

across the wide web that connects the tachometer and clock. The low-profile version has no web at all, and the instruments are located lower and father apart.

Each style was designed for a specific application. Hooded Rally-Pacs were used on all 1964½ Mustangs and most 1965s. In fact, the hooded version was optional for all 1965 Mustangs with the Falcon-style warning light instrument panel. In the spring of 1965, when the GT Equipment Group and the Decor Interior options were introduced with

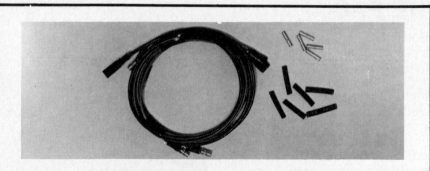

Here's how you can determine which Rally-Pac is correct for your Mustang: If your car is a 1964½ or a standard 1965 with the Falcon-style warning light instrument panel (top), then you need the hooded Rally-Pac. If your Mustang uses the 5-dial gauge-type instrument panel (bottom — all 1966s, and 1965s with the GT Equipment Group and/or Decor Interior), then look for the low-profile Rally-Pac.

WIRE REPAIR KIT

Rally-Pacs are often found with the wire leads snipped, the result of some hasty removal. But cut wires do not render a Rally-Pac useless. A Rally-Pac Wire Repair Kit can be added, even if only a small portion of the original wires remain. The kit contains 6 wires (with the correct male/female ends), 6 crimp butt connectors, and 6 heat shrink insulators. You simply strip ¼" of insulation from each wire, slip the bare ends of both the new and old wires into the metal connectors, crimp the connectors with a crimper or pliers, slide the insulators over the connectors, and heat the insulators with a match or cigarette lighter. The insulation will shrink tightly over the connector. Voila! Your Rally-Pac will hook up just like new.

their new gauge-type instrument panel, the low-profile Rally-Pac was released to compliment the new instrument layout. And since the gauge-type instrument panel became standard on all 1966 Mustangs, the hooded Rally-Pac was discontinued and the low-profile version took over.

Simply put, warning light instrument panels got the hooded Rally-Pac and gauge-type instrument panels got the low-profile.

To complicate matters further, 3 different tachometers designed for specific engine use came with each Rally-Pac style, which gives us 6 very specific Rally-Pacs, as follows:

Hooded Style:
6,000 rpm...6 cylinder
6,000 rpm...8 cylinder
8,000 rpm...8 cylinder (289 High Performance)

Low-Profile Style:
6,000 rpm...6 cylinder
6,000 rpm...8 cylinder
8,000 rpm...8 cylinder (289 High Performance)

To determine a 6,000 rpm tach's cylinder usage (6 or 8), remove the 2 screws from the rear of the housing and carefully slide the tachometer unit out. On the back of the unit, look for the stamping "6 cyl." or "8 cyl". Of

course, all 8,000 rpm tachometers are 8 cylinder units which can be used with any V-8 engine, although they were originally installed only in 289 High Performance Mustangs. Connecting a 6 cylinder tachometer to a V-8 engine will lead to a higher rpm reading.

TESTING

If you're buying a used Rally-Pac, it's wise to check the unit's operation before closing the deal. Fortunately, both the clock and the tach can be tested very simply. Look for 6 wires emerging from the Rally-Pac assembly — 3 from the tachometer and 3 from the clock. If you're lucky, the wires will still be intact and uncut, but many units were removed from cars by simply snipping the wires. Before testing, you'll need to

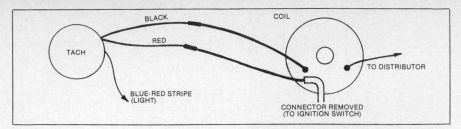

Unlike a dwell tachometer, the Rally-Pac tach operates in series with the coil, or between the coil and ignition. To test, simply connect the wires as shown in the above diagram.

The engine used for tach testing doesn't have to be a 1965-66 Mustang; in fact, you can use a coil from any car. We found that 1967 and later Ford cars work more conveniently because of their push-on type connections; simply remove the coil's ignition wire, push the black tachometer wire onto the coil post, and plug the red tach wire into the female-type ignition connector (arrow).

know which wires go where, as follows:

Tachometer Side:
Blue w/red stripe: light
Red: ignition switch
Black: coil

Clock:
Blue w/red stripe: light
Black: ground
Blue w/black stripe: hot

TESTING THE TACH. To check tachometer operation, simply place the tach in series with the coil from outside the engine compartment. Disconnect the wire to the ignition side of the coil, then connect the black tachometer wire to the coil and the red wire to the disconnected factory wire. Start the engine and watch for correct tachometer action.

If the tach needle does not move, double-check your connections. If the needle still fails to wiggle, remove the tachometer unit from the Rally-Pac housing, then carefully remove the clear plastic lens by prying up 3 prongs. The tachometer will then slip out of its housing. Check the internal wiring for breaks and shorts. If there is nothing visably wrong, the tach may require repair by an instrument repair shop. Many of the Mustang vendors offer a Rally-Pac tach repair service.

TESTING THE CLOCK. Compared to the tachometer, the Rally-Pac clock is a relatively simple device. To test it, simply ground the black wire and touch the hot wire (blue w/black stripe) to the positive battery post. If the clock does not run, don't fret; you can probably repair it yourself. In the same manner outlined above for the tachometer, remove the clock mechanism from its case. Basically, the clock is wound by a

Like most automotive clocks, the Rally-Pac utilizes a set of points (arrow) to wind the clock mechanism.

set of points; as the spring winds down, the points make contact and an electrical charge jolts the upper point upward, winding the clock spring. That's the click you hear every couple of minutes. In most cases, a non-functioning clock can be repaired by applying a small amount of clock oil (3-in-1 oil works good, too) to the

PAINTING THE PAC

Both the hooded and the low-profile Rally-Pacs use a wrinkle paint on the metal exterior parts. Unfortunately, the wrinkle in the wrinkle paints found at parts houses does not match the original finish. However, Eddie Caheely of the Mustang Stable has hit upon a combination that uses an easy-to-find brand wrinkle paint and your wife's oven.

The Rally-Pac must be completely disassembled before beginning the paint process since you'll be painting only the metal parts with the wrinkle finish. Use paint stripper to remove all the old paint, then spray the Rally-Pac with VHT wrinkle paint, which is available only in black. Be sure to coat the parts evenly; thicker paint will wrinkle differently. Set the oven on warm, place the freshly painted Rally-Pac on an old baking sheet, and bake the pieces for approximately 30 minutes. Use the 30 minutes only as a guide; keep checking the oven until the texture appears close to the original, then remove the Rally-Pac.

Some low-profile Rally-Pacs in 1966 were color-keyed to the interior color. In that case, the black wrinkle paint can be lightly coated with the correct color paint. Use just enough paint to cover the black completely because too much paint will fill in the wrinkle finish.

Rally-Pac clock testing can be accomplished quite easily. Just ground the black wire and touch the hot wire (blue w/black stripe) to the positive battery post.

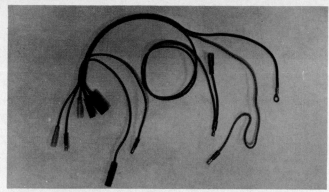

A Rally-Pac wiring harness is available from most Mustang merchants. And don't forget the wire channel that neatly routes the Rally-Pac wires under the dash on low-profile versions.

Most non-functioning clocks can be repaired by oiling the gear and winding mechanisms. Clock oil is preferred, but 3-In-1 will get the job done also.

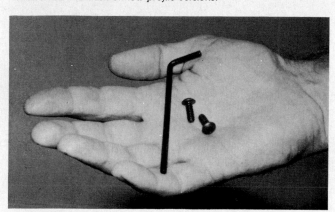

New tamper-proof screws are also available from Mustang dealers. Be sure to specify 1965 or 1966 since the screws differ. An installation tool is included.

bearings, easing the internal friction caused by drying. Pitted or worn points can also create problems; you can try filing down high spots with an ignition point file or an emery board. If that doesn't work, the points may need replacing.

INSTALLING THE RALLY-PAC

Before installing the Rally-Pac, you'll need to purchase a Rally-Pac wiring harness from one of the Mustang parts merchants. This harness will connect the Rally-Pac wires to the underdash wiring harness. Since detailed instructions are included with the Rally-Pac harness, we won't go into specific details here. The installation requires removal of the instrument panel and the driver's side kick panel, otherwise the installation can be described as find-the-right-wires-and-hook-them-up. Following the instructions closely, any Mustanger should be able to install his own Rally-Pac.

Tamper-proof Rally-Pac installation screws are currently available from most Mustang parts merchants. An installation tool is also supplied. And don't forget the wiring channel that routes the Rally-Pac wires on the low-profile version. The channels are also sold through most Mustang vendors.

FACE TO FACE

Two different tach faces appear on low-profile, 8,000 rpm Rally-Pacs, for no known reason other than readability. On one, the numbers read in increments of ten, the other in increments of five. Both can be considered correct.

RALLY-PAC PRICES*

1965:

6000 rpm for six cylinder	$375.00
6000 rpm for V-8	$250.00
8000 rpm for V-8	$300.00

1966 (or 1965 with GT Equipment Group or Decor Interior):

6000 rpm for six cylinder	$350.00
6000 rpm for V-8	$350.00
8000 rpm for V-8	$400.00

*Prices taken for the 1982 Edition "Mustang Value Guide". All prices listed here are based on clean units in working condition.

How To
REPLACE YOUR MUSTANG'S INTERIOR

by Howard Buck

Six months ago, if someone had told me I would be sitting here writing this article, it would have crossed my mind that they probably paddled in circles a lot.

I used to be one of those guys who, when he found out you were into Mustangs, bored you to death about the '66 coupe I bought in 1966, drove into the ground, and sold for only $300 in 1972 thinking I had squeezed every last ounce of usefulness from its semi-mangled frame.

My only interest in the classic pony was that it brought back some good memories of my college days and sparked a bit of nostalgia when I thought of how I used to perform my mechanical work. I swore that I would never ever touch a greasy place on an automobile again if I ever got to a point where I could rationalize paying someone else to do it, afford it or not.

Fate started to take its course in September of 1979 while I was a free lance art and advertising consultant here in Lakeland. I was approached by Larry Dobbs and asked to help establish a format for his up-and-coming Mustang Monthly Magazine. Sure, I said, just as long as I don't have to mess with cars and get greasy. He agreed and the seed was planted.

For the next 17 months I managed to work with the magazine and all its projects at arm's length, keeping myself detached from the affixation that Larry and his associates had for talking about old Mustangs and all the technical jargon that was in the magazine to lure new subscribers. After all, why would I need to know any of that stuff -- I was just there to take words and pictures and

transform them into a magazine once a month.

Then the plot thickened. (I'm convinced this whole thing has been conspiracy to get me addicted to all this craziness). I came to work with Mustang Monthly full time in March of this year as Advertising Director. Well...that meant I had to be around Mustangs and the strange folks usually found in the near vicinity for eight hours a day

I suppose they all knew that anyone who had owned a Mustang for six years couldn't keep his invisible protective shield up forever, and they were right. The second Monday morning at work, Larry mentioned he had bought a "nice" little '66 coupe over the weekend and asked if I could pick it up that afternoon because he had other business to tend to. Boy did he have my number!

I used to be one of those guys who bored you to death about the '66 coupe I bought in 1966, drove into the ground, and sold for only $300 in 1972 . . .

When I picked up the car, it turned out to be, except for the color, just like my old reliable pony. This was your basic Mustang, a 1966 coupe, 200 cu.in. 6 cyl., 3 speed manual transmission, and a radio. I climbed in and proceeded to drive 20 miles back to Lakeland.

It was like turning back the hands of time. All the old familiar noises that old Mustangs make were there. The gear shift rattled, the clutch chattered in first, the brakes squeaked and the fan belt made a terrible squealing noise when you drove through a mud puddle. Wow! What a case of dejavu; I felt like I was back in Ft. Lauderdale on my way home from Jr. College.

When I returned to the shop, I was met by a boss with a grin that would make a cheshire cat envious. "How'd ya like it" he said with a twinkle in his eye. "Brings back a lot of memories" I said, "What you gonna do with it." "Depends," he said. "On what," I asked. "On whether or not you buy it..."

The trap was sprung and I was caught...hook, line and sinker; but there was one huge obstacle in the way. I had to convince my wife that I should buy an old car that needed work, that we couldn't afford, and that we didn't need for transportation. How was I going to convince her we should buy the same kind of car that used to make me scream and curse and lay in the driveway kicking my feet when I was trying to fix something.

All the way home I planned my defense and prepared myself for battle. I pulled in the drive quietly and tiptoed up the walk so she wouldn't hear me coming and get a chance to fire the first volley. I walked in, greeted her with a big kiss and said, "come see what I brought home." "Oh, no," she said, "it's not a Mustang, is it?" "Just come see," I said, as I pulled her toward the front door.

We walked out and the unexpected happened. She showed signs of experiencing the same nostalgic feelings I did. I could see old memories flashing through her eyes, like our first date and when the old pony was decorated for our honeymoon.

I struck while she was at her weakest point..."I'm gonna buy it." There was a pause, and then she sighed, "I knew you'd have one sooner or later." The next thing I knew, I was up to my ears in grease, gunk, and spray paint, and Donald Farr, our editor, was next to me, instead of my wife, showing me how to clean my engine compartment for an article in the June magazine.

When we finished with the engine, I felt a strange burst of enthusiasm and pride emerging from my body. I had actually enjoyed myself. Could it be that I have been struck by the never-ending urge to make my Mustang showroom perfect?? My mind was racing...let's see, I have an income tax check coming back -- what can I buy?

The check arrived and, after a quick tour through the Mustang Monthly display ads, I made my decision. I had just enough money to buy all the goodies necessary to redo my interior - if I did the work myself.

The next day, Donald asked if I had any ideas for a "How To" article for the July magazine. "Sure," I said slyly, "we could redo the interior of my car and I'll write a story on How To Make Your Inferior Interior Superior and live to tell about it." Surprisingly, he agreed, and I ordered the parts.

By the time the parts arrived, our copy deadline was near, so Donald and I recruited the assistance of our able-bodied cameraman and production assistant, John Summerlin, for expediency. Most of the project, however, can be done by one person except in several instances where a second pair of hands come in very handy.

You'll need to sacrifice the use of your car for two or three days if you drive yours everyday like I do, and you'll also need the following list of materials.

1. A good set of tools, including sockets, and a variety of screwdrivers.
2. 000 steel wool.
3. Allen wrenches.

4. Color matched spray paint for your dash, kick panels (if you're not going to replace them), rear seat side panels, and door panels (this paint is available at several suppliers in the magazine.)
5. Masking tape and newspaper.
6. Wire cutters.
7. Hog rings and hog ring pliers.
8. A razor knife.
9. All the pieces you intend to replace. In my case, this included new seat covers (I would recommend that you buy both front and rear seat covers even if the back is in good condition, as there is likely to be a disappointing color mismatch due to 10-15 years of age and fading. This would not apply to black seats. I also bought new door panels, arm rest assemblies, front and rear carpet, and the instrument bezel.
10. A copy of "How To Restore Your Mustang" and a shop manual are extremely helpful, but not absolutely necessary.
11. A lot of patience and the desire to do a good job.

Now you are ready to begin. Disconnect the battery. BE SURE to establish a system of keeping parts and screws together, as this can become a big problem at re-assembly time. Paper lunch bags work well.

Interior disassembly can begin with any part and doesn't have to follow any specific order, although some items must be removed before others. Our order of disassembly should easily guide you through the dismantling process, however, some steps may be switched around for the sake of convenience.

First, remove the steering wheel center. On my '66 coupe, this was done by simply pushing down and turning to the left before the lifting off.

Next, it is advisable for convenience sake to remove the steering wheel. This is done by removing the steering wheel attaching nut and using a steering wheel puller to remove the wheel. Some steering wheels will pull of by hand; ours did not, so we left it on and worked around it.

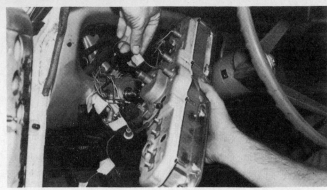

Next, remove the instrument cluster. Reach under and behind the dash and unscrew the speedometer cable from the speedometer. Remove the retaining screws and tilt the instrument cluster out. The plugs and wiring may be code labeled to avoid confusion when reinstalling. Masking tape or paint works well.

Now you are ready for the glove box door and liner to come out. With the glove box open, disconnect the retaining wire on 65-66 models. Remove the hinge attaching screws, and store the hinge with the door.

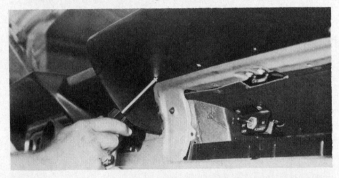

Next comes the instrument panel safety pad. For 1965's, remove right and left side lower chrome mouldings. For 1966, remove underside retaining screws.

Remove the screws that attach the garnish mouldings at the base of windshield. Remove the radio speaker grill, unplug speaker wires, and lift speaker out.

Use needle-nose pliers to remove the defroster duct retaining clips and lift out the ducts.

Remove the nuts holding the pad to the dash. On '66 models, 2 nuts at either end of pad must be removed.

Also, there is a third nut in the speaker well in the center of the dash that must come out. Use care when removing the pad itself, as it may be stuck and possibly tear.

So much for the instrument panel at this point. Next, we need to get the front seats out of the way, up until now, they have been left in for convenience.

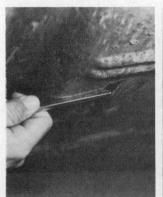

Use a screwdriver from beneath the car to remove the 4 floorpan plugs to gain access to the seat track retaining bolts. Use a ½" deepwell socket and extension to remove the nut.

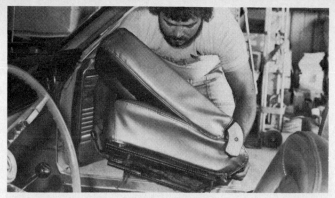

Lift the seat from the car.

Remove the four metal seat track to carpet pads and store until reassembly.

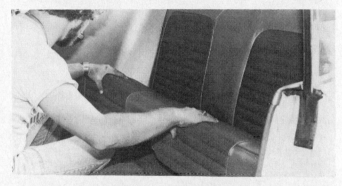

Now for the back seats. This should take only a couple of minutes. First, push in and lift out the seat bottom and remove it from the car.

Next, remove the two rear seat back retaining bolts at the base of the seat, lift up and out on the seat back and remove it from the car. Also, remove the rear deck from between the rear seat and rear window.

Back to the dash panel. Pull off the radio control knobs and remove the radio to dash retaining nuts. Disconnect antenna wire, radio lead wire, and light wire. Remove the nut that retains the radio to the support bracket. Lower the radio out through the bottom of the dash.

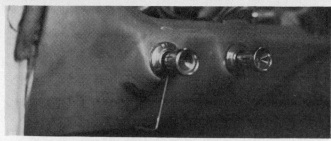

The windshield wiper knob is fastened by an Allen screw - remove and store it. Remove the cigarette lighter.

The light switch is next...turn it to the "on" position. Reach under the dash and find the rear of the switch assembly, press the knob release button, and remove the headlight knob and shaft.

From this point forward, we chose to mask the rest of the chrome parts on the dash for expediency.

Above the dash, remove the rearview mirror and sun visors for cleaning and polishing later.

Remove the step plates by removing the screws on the top and sides. Also remove the windlacing along the door pillars.

Now you can remove the kick panels. Remove the two screws that hold each one on, then slide the panel toward the rear of the car and set aside for cleaning and painting at a later time. When replacing the kick panels, make sure you don't tighten the screws too tight, as this will crack the panel.

Remove the rear interior quarter panels which are held on by 3 screws each. Set them aside for future cleaning and painting.

My headliner was in excellent condition, so I chose not to replace it, but if yours is being replaced, it comes out next. You can cut the fabric along the edge of the windshield and back window weatherstrips, then peel the headlining from the right and left sides in the package tray area and from the roof side rails. Remove the headliner and bows from the roof. Be sure to keep the bows in sequence and replace them in the car as soon as they are removed from the headliner.

Ok, lets get the grubby old carpet out of there. First, remove the front seat belts.

Next, remove the 2 carpet retaining screws from the floor pans, located on the front seat mounting pan near the door opening.

Remove the chrome trim from around the shift lever and remove the 2 carpet sections from the car.

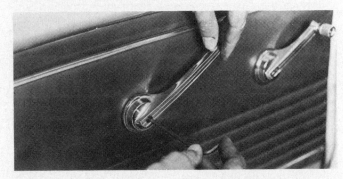

Don't forget your door panels. First, remove the door and window handles with an Allen wrench (some models used a clip or screw).

Next, remove the arm rests using a large Phillips-head screwdriver.

The only thing left is the door panel itself. Use a screwdriver to pry the door clips from the door frame, then very carefully pop the door panel loose and set it aside.

Well, we're as far as we need to go in the disassembly phase. If you've been good...you should have all your parts organized and cataloged. If you've been bad...it probably looks like the bomb went off in your garage. At this point, it's wise to conduct an intermediate clean-up and organizing session.

Now it's time for the seat refinishing, the most involved and tedious part of the entire project.

You'll need a good work surface, preferably counter or table top height.

First, lay a front seat on its side and remove the outside chrome trim, then remove the hairpin that attaches the seat back. Repeat on the other side.

Be sure not to lose the chrome seat trim attaching clip.

Pry the bracket over the seat cushion stud.

Remove the seat back and take the position adjusting bolt from the bottom. Remove the stop plate from the top of the seat bottom.

Place the seat bottom upside down on the table and remove the springs to release the tension on the track. Now remove the front 2 track attaching screws, slide the track forward, and remove the 2 rear screws. Then remove the track.

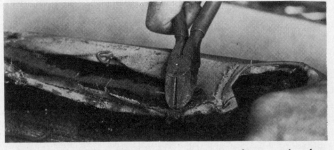

Using wire cutters, remove the hog rings from each edge of the seat.

Remove the retaining wire from the edge of the seat and set aside for reassembly.

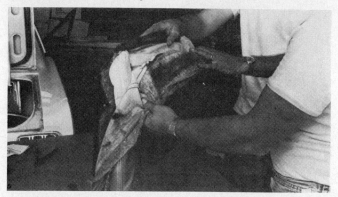

Fold the seat cover edges over the seat frame; the cover will be attached to the center.

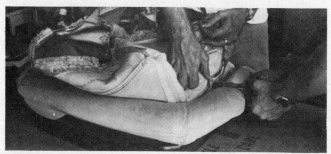

Remove the hog rings from the seat center and remove the hog ring retaining wires. This will enable you to remove the seat cover.

Place the seat back upside down on the table and remove the back board by prying it up with a screwdriver. Now pop the clips loose like you did on the door panels. Next, remove the staples holding the upholstery on the masonite and peel the material off. To remove the seat cover from the seat back cushion, follow the same steps used on the seat bottom.

The rear seat covers can be removed by simply cutting the hog rings underneath.

To recover the seats, you will need hog rings and hog ring pliers. These can be purchased at a good hardware store.

Make sure your new upholstery is warm (the best way to heat it is to leave it in the sun for awhile. This will help prevent tearing when you are stretching it over the seat).

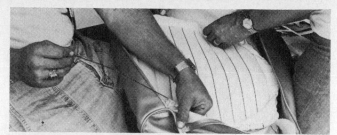

Now, re-install the retaining wires in the new seat cover.

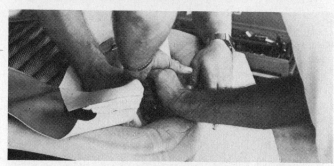

Fasten the center portion of the seat cover in place with hog rings.

Pull the cover over the frame edges and fasten. This is where most wrinkles will occur; they must be smoothed out. Re-connect the seat cover to the underside with new hog rings.

Install the seat back adjusting screw and stop plate.

To recover the front seat back board, several steps need to be followed. First, remove the retaining clips. Next, using a spray adhesive, attach a thin layer of foam rubber (or heavyweight polyester pellon interfacing) to the outside of the backboard.

Finding staples small enough to restaple the upholstery to the back board may be difficult. If they are unavailable in your area, use 3M Weather Stripping Adhesive and follow the instructions on the tube. Now replace the retaining clips and put the back board on the seat back.

Clean the seat tracks of all dirt and rust, and repaint black. Install tracks. Reassemble the seat back to the seat bottom and install clips and side mouldings. When you've completed the seat covers installation, it's time to set up for repainting the parts that need it. In my case, I repainted the rear inside quarterpanels, the rear window deck, the inside door skin, kick panels, and dash board.

All these pieces need to be cleaned and sanded before painting. All but the dash and door skins can be spread out on paper and sprayed using matching spray paint in aeresol cans (available from several suppliers advertised in the magazine).

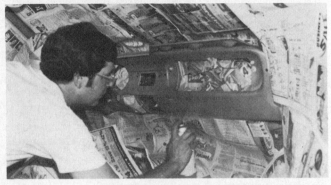

When masking the dash and door skins, be very thorough. Overspray from paint cans is very persistent stuff, and can get into the smallest opening. A little extra time here is well spent.

Now spray the dash and door skins. Do not try to completely cover surfaces on the first coat, as this will probably cause runs. Several thin coats will be more effective with a short drying time between coats.

While the paint is drying, it's a good time to start polishing all the chrome pieces. Use 000 steel wool and a good dose of elbow grease. The more time you spend here the better the chrome will look.

The instrument bezel is next. Remove the retaining screws on the back that hold the bezel to instruments and separate. Clean the plastic lens with window cleaner and rejoin the new bezel to instruments.

Believe it or not, we're coming into the home stretch. From this point forward, you just re-install all the pieces you took off in reverse order. You'll be astounded as you watch the inside of your car transform into a virtual showpiece. This is undoubtly the most satisfactory portion of the project.

When all the finishing touches have been completed, there is nothing left to do but brag about how great a job you did because you will have a truly superior interior.

How To
REPLACE YOUR MUSTANG HEADLINER

By Art Mullins

Mustang owners are a notoriously finicky lot. One item guaranteed to turn off a ponycar fan is a ragged and grungy headliner. Unfortunately, the chances of a Mustang reaching teenage with a perfect headliner are roughly the same as the Arabs giving away free oil — very slim. Headliners draw catastrophe like sugar draws flies.

If your headliner has been a casualty, take heart, all is not lost. Mustang headliners are still available from many of the advertisers in this magazine and most auto upholstery shops can make up a headliner for your pet ponycar in a jiffy. The going rate for a tailor-made headliner is about the same as a NOS model.

This reporter had occasion to replace a headliner recently in a '67 Mustang coupe. One local firm, Seatco, Inc. of Arlington, VA consistently draws favorable reports for work performed on cars belonging to members of the National Capital Region Mustang Club, of which this correspondent is a member. A quick phone call to the manager, an appointment was made, permission to photograph the transplant was cheerfully given '67 Mustang coupe was taken to the shop.

Frank Padgett, a Seatco craftsman with more than 35 years auto trim experience, was given the job and right off the bat I was told by Frank: "Mustangs are one of the hardest cars to install a headliner in, next to the VW Bug. The rear window has to come out to do a decent job and there's very little room to move around in. Big cars are easier."

Frank set to work. First, the deck lid was covered with one-inch foam rubber to protect the newly-painted finish. Then the chrome trim around the rear window was removed and stored on a nearby table in the order in which it was removed. Next, the rear window was removed by the novel method of Frank lying in the Mustang's back seat and pushing outward with his feet

as a helper held onto the window.

With the rear window out, Frank removed both sections of the back seat. Next the package tray was removed. Moving to the front of the little hoss, the inside quarter panels were removed, followed by the coat hangers and dome light, windshield quarterpost moldings, rearview mirror and sunvisors, windlace and scuff plates. Frank works quickly, with the ease of long practice and nary a wasted movement.

Then it was the moment of truth: removal of the old headliner by cutting from the rear and carefully marking the bows as they were withdrawn. To make sure there's no mistake, Frank marks the bows with chalk as they come out of the side rails.

The bows are then inserted into the new headliner which was placed on a clean worktable. Adhesive is sprayed on the inside of the headliner where it fits around the rear window. The liner was then placed in position with the roof bows in the side rails. More adhesive was applied to the back side of the liner and the area at the front windshield weatherstrip. The headliner was then tucked under the weatherstripping after excess material was trimmed away. Ditto for about six inches down each windshield quarterpost (A pillars), where the liner is held in place by retainers on each post.

More adhesive is sprayed on the back of the liner and on the roof side rails and door openings. Here again it was smoothed and excess liner material was trimmed off with a razor blade. The headliner is held in place at the rear corners beside the package tray by metal prongs.

The adhesive used was Parabond, a professional use product sprayed out of a five gallon can and unavailable to the average mortal driveway Mustang trimmer. A good adhesive is marketed by 3-M for general upholstery use and is available at most parts stores in spray cans.

Nearing the homestretch, and following roughly the same se-

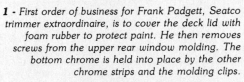

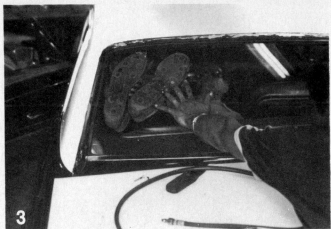

1 - First order of business for Frank Padgett, Seatco trimmer extraordinaire, is to cover the deck lid with foam rubber to protect paint. He then removes screws from the upper rear window molding. The bottom chrome is held into place by the other chrome strips and the molding clips.

2 - Frank then cleans dried and old sealer from around rubber molding on the rear window. This makes for a neater job and often the sealer — although more than 13 years old — is still gooey enough to stick to paint. And clothes. And hair.

3 - We've all seen baby shoes handing from the rear view mirror, but size 11s in a rear window? Actually Frank is lying on his back inside on the rear seat which is still inside the car and pushing on the rear window with his feet from the inside. Frank explains sneakers flex and distribute the outward pressure and prevent damage to the window. And there's another reason: he's not so tired after a day of hopping in and out of cars with light shoes.

quence in reverse as the removal; windshield quarter post moldings were replaced, as were the sunvisors and rear view mirror. Then came the coat hangers, dome light, rear interior quarter panels, windlace in the door openings and scuff plates, leaving the package tray and the rear seat back and bottom to be installed.

The rear window had come out without the rubber molding, which was then pulled away along with a pound or so of old sealer. The molding was carefully sealed back around the window glass in an interior groove provided in the molding. A strong draw cord is placed in a large outer groove in the molding. The window, molding and cord is placed in position by pushing and a few healthy slaps with the open hand. When the window and molding is in place, the cord is pulled which pulls the inside flange of the molding inward and down over the newly installed headliner. This is an operation that has to be seen to be appreciated.

While the package tray was out we decided to cover it with material matching the Moonskin headliner. The package tray has withstood the sun of 14 Virginia summers and looked like nine miles of bad road. If the car is to be kept 100 per cent stock, now is the time to paint the faded tray.

The package tray was then installed, droopy insulation behind the rear seat was reglued and put into place, and the rear seat sections were installed after blowing out the car interior with compressed air.

Rear window chrome molding was replaced after sealing the window. The clip retainers for the molding were replaced then the bottom molding was snapped on, followed by the sides and then the top piece. If the clip retainers are broken, rusted or

unuseable, replacements can be found at any auto glass shop.

That about buttoned up the headliner project. Time for the job? About two and a half hours with time out for a pizza.

"We feel that in order to do a top-notch job the rear window must be removed to tuck the headliner in securely. It's been our experience that pushing the headliner under the rear window molding is not enough to hold it," says Neal Ailstock, amiable Seatco co-manager.

"Since the increase in interest in early Mustangs in the past few years, we work on about a dozen Mustangs a week, that's about 10 or 12 per cent of our business," explains Ailstock. "We make up headliners for a lot of people, there's nothing especially hard about it. Any good shop can do it."

Material is included for the recovering of sunvisors in the factory headliners, but the process is complicated. Despite repeated scrubbings with a variety of cleaners, the old visors do not match the new headliner color. Years of cigarette and cigar smoke have taken their toll.

Would I attempt the installation of a headliner myself? Yes. A big consideration is the size of your bankroll and it obviously is not a job for the rank amateur, but for anyone who is handy around a Mustang it should be a job within his capability — with a helper. The job requires a minimum of tools and equipment and I feel a magazine pictorial guide or detailed instructions are a must. I do not think the Mustang shop manual instructions are detailed enough, even with the drawings.

The new headliner dramatically improves the car's appearance but there's another pleasant surprise — the whole car smells new!

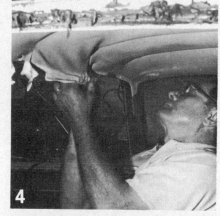

1 - Frank carefully removes the rubber window molding after clearing away old sealer. Often the window molding is brittle and unuseable — in which case new molding must be used. This is still available from many advertisers in Mustang Monthly.

2 - The package tray and interior quarter panels are among the first items to be removed from this '67 Mustang coupe.

3 - The next item to be removed is the windshield quarter post molding.

4 - Frank prefers to start the old headliner removal at the rear of the car. He cuts carefully and works his way to the front of the car, removing the bows as he goes.

5 - The rear of the car with the headliner removed.

6 - The old headliner is free except for the windshield molding.

7 - The bows are inserted in the new headliner, taking care to get them in the right order. Just so there will be no mistake, Frank uses colored chalk to make his own markings. Most headliner bows are marked at the factory but the markings often fade.

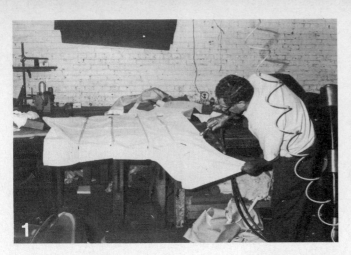

1 - The new headliner is sprayed on the inside with a professional adhesive, Parabond.

2 - Frank sprays adhesive to the side areas above the driver's seat. He uses a cardboard mask to control the overspray. For do-it-yourselfers, a very good general purpose 3-M upholstery adhesive is available in spray cans.

3 - The new headliner partially in place. The sides have yet to be attached.

4 - Adhesive is sprayed on the area over the package tray behind the passenger's seat.

5 - Headliner is tucked into the area normally occupied by the rear window. This is the big reason the window was removed.

6 - Excess headliner is trimmed away with scissors and/or razors.

7 - Tucking in the headliner before installing the windlace.

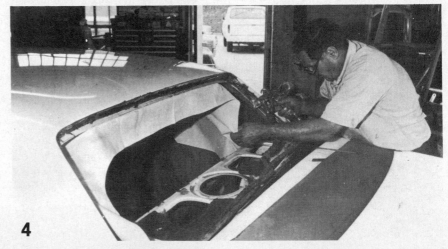

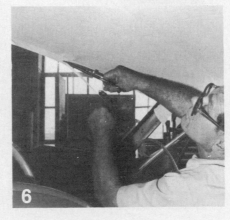

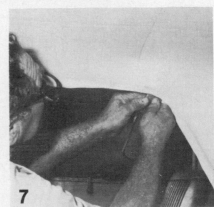

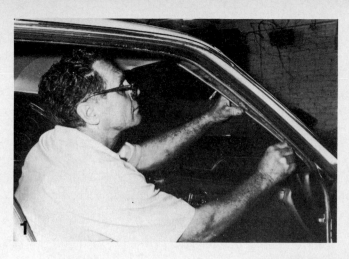

1 - Windshield quarterpost molding is replaced.

2 - A bit more cleaning in the rear window area before re-installation.

3 - The rubber molding is carefully placed back on the rear window glass.

4 - A plastic cord is placed in the molding groove prior to installation of the window. Once installed, the cord is pulled causing the molding to snap exactly into place, a tricky operation that must be seen to be appreciated.

5 - A helper is needed to hold and push the glass and molding into place.

6 - The fit of the glass is checked to make sure it's tight. The chrome trim is ready to be attached after sealer is applied to rear window.

7 - Package tray is screwed into place.

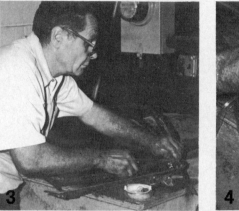

CONSOLE YOURSELF
How To Refinish And Install Mustang Consoles

by Donald Farr

The 1965-66 Mustang console was certainly a versatile piece of optional equipment. With only one tooling, Ford managed to fit the same console into every bucket seat model — hardtop and convertible, air conditioned and non-air conditioned, automatic and 4-speed, standard interior and Decor interior. It was all a matter of various trims and a little hacksaw work.

Hacksaw work? At Ford Motor Company? Well, not really, but the standard console base, which was installed in non-air conditioned hardtops and fastbacks, was cut to serve various functions. For example, convertible consoles required a "notching" to fit the reinforced floor, and the storage compartment up front was sliced off completely to make room for the optional under-dash air conditioning unit.

Now, we can't envision some assembly line worker spending his 8 hour shift trimming consoles with a hacksaw, so we assume (because we don't know for sure) that the consoles were modified by the supplier (or suppliers) to Ford's specifications. Ford,

in all probability, ordered consoles from the supplier by shape — short or long, and/or convertibles or non-convertible. And we doubt that the supplier used hacksaws either; the consoles were probably trimmed on some fancy cutting machine.

To add to the confusion further, the console top configuration depended upon transmission type and, sometimes, interior style. Manual transmission cars got a rectangular hole in the console top for the shifter boot, while automatic versions received dual rectangular slots

for the shifter and the shift selector pattern. With the standard interior, the strips on either edge of the console top were painted camera-case black. It would seem logical that Decor Interior consoles got the woodgrain treatment, but that isn't necessarily the case. *Some* 1965-66 Mustangs equipped with both the Decor Interior and console received the woodgrain strips, but not all.

Confusing? It sure is! In all, the console combinations for early Mustangs totals 16, as follows:

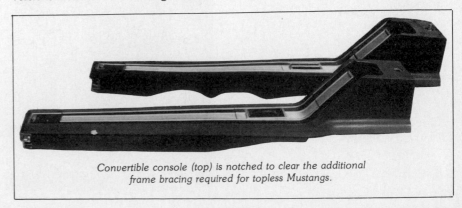

Convertible console (top) is notched to clear the additional frame bracing required for topless Mustangs.

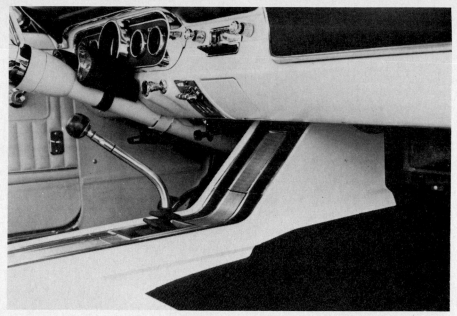

Non-air conditioned Mustangs have a convenient storage compartment up front.

In 1965-66, the Mustang air conditioner mounted below the dash, so the console's storage compartment was removed. Chrome trim covered the console's forward section.

Air conditioning console chrome trim varies from 1965 to 1966. The 1965 trim is narrower, about 1" wide at the bottom, while the 1966 trim grew to 3".

COUPE OR FASTBACK:
Automatic:
   standard short console
   standard long console
   woodgrain short console
   woodgrain long console
4-speed:
   standard short console
   standard long console
   woodgrain short console
   woodgrain long console

CONVERTIBLE:
Automatic:
   standard short console
   standard long console
   woodgrain short console
   woodgrain long console
4-speed:
   standard short console
   standard long console
   woodgrain short console
   woodgrain long console

Short consoles (the ones for air conditioned cars) were trimmed with a chrome end piece to cover the cut plastic. Again, Ford complicated the matter by changing the trim at the end of 1965. The 1965 piece was about 1 inch wide at the base and tapered slightly at the top. In 1966, the end trim's base was nearly 3 inches wide and tapered sharply toward the top.

Confusion reigned in the Ford dealer's service department, too. Replacement consoles were supplied full-length and uncut for convertible application, so the service dealer had to modify the console himself for the particular Mustang involved. Fortunately, Ford supplied instructions and a template for the trimming operations — or we'd see some mighty weird looking consoles today.

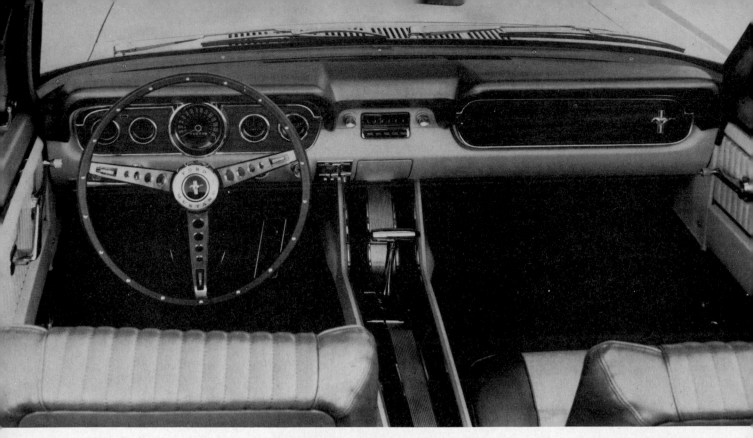

Some, but not all, Interior Decor-equipped Mustangs got the woodgrain strips on the console. The strips matched the woodgrain on the instrument panel and glove compartment.

Console tops depended on transmission type. Automatic shifters have a dual slot for the shifter and the shift selector indicator, while manual shifters require only one larger rectangular hole.

Example: Say a 1965 Mustang owner wanted to add the console to his air conditioned convertible. Generally, if he wasn't the resourceful do-it-yourself sort, he would return the Mustang to his Ford dealer's service department for the console installation. The parts manager would order the correct color console base and other assorted pieces and trim items (the console top and shifter plates were specified by transmission and interior type; the ash tray, lights, and various attaching screws were also ordered separately). Then, using the 23½"x29½" template supplied with the console base, the service department would trim the plastic base to fit the convertible's floor and remove the forward storage compartment for air conditioning clearance. The chrome end trim was not supplied with the console; it too had to be ordered separately. That's why you'll see some convertible consoles without the trim; either the parts manager was ignorant of its existence or the car owner didn't want to pay extra for it.

Today's '65 and '66 Mustang owners can perform the same operation when adding a standard hardtop/fastback console to a convertible or air conditioned model (see "Convertible Console Installation" and "Air Conditioning, Too" sidebar). Trouble is, a console trimmed for a convertible will not properly fit a hardtop or fastback (there will be gaps between the console and the carpet). And a console cut for air conditioning will appear too short in a non-air conditioned application.

Convertible Console Installation

Most of the consoles found at swap meets and junk yards fit hardtop and fastback Mustangs - without the required "notching" for convertibles. Modifying the console for a convertible is a simple operation, especially now since Jim Osborn has reproduced the 23½"x29½" template originally supplied with replacement consoles. Use the template to scribe the notching pattern on the console, then trim the base with a coping saw.

The template is available from: Jim Osborn Reproductions, 3070 Briarcliff Road NE, Atlanta, Georgia 30329. Price was not available at this printing.

If you're working in cold weather, warm the plastic by holding the console near a heater or fire.

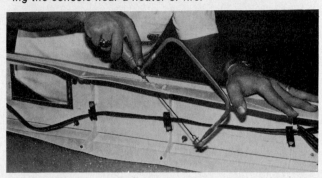

Carefully trim the plastic with a coping saw, found at most hardware stores. The thin-bladed saw will easily cut around the curves.

Using the template available from Jim Osborn Reproductions, scribe the notching pattern on the console base.

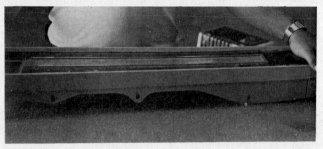

The finished product. You may want to smooth the edges with fine sandpaper.

AIR CONDITIONING, TOO?

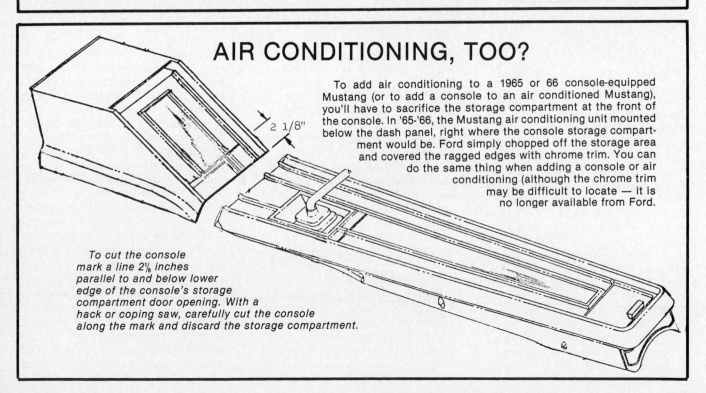

To add air conditioning to a 1965 or 66 console-equipped Mustang (or to add a console to an air conditioned Mustang), you'll have to sacrifice the storage compartment at the front of the console. In '65-'66, the Mustang air conditioning unit mounted below the dash panel, right where the console storage compartment would be. Ford simply chopped off the storage area and covered the ragged edges with chrome trim. You can do the same thing when adding a console or air conditioning (although the chrome trim may be difficult to locate — it is no longer available from Ford.

2 1/8"

To cut the console mark a line 2⅛ inches parallel to and below lower edge of the console's storage compartment door opening. With a hack or coping saw, carefully cut the console along the mark and discard the storage compartment.

How To
INSTALL MUSTANG CARPET

by Jerry Heasley

TYPES OF CARPET

Generally, you can buy two types of carpet for your Mustang: "standard" or "molded". What most dealers refer to as standard carpet is nowhere near like stock replacement. It is cut and sewn, but not molded. It lays flat until you install and fit it in the car, when you must lay it out so that it conforms to the shape of your floorboard. Of course, it is cheaper than the molded, and it does have a market, which is why we see it for sale. There are some Mustang drivers who prefer a usable rug, and care nothing about stock specs. Like a used car dealer who plans to sell the Mustang anyway. But we do not recommend these rugs for you, if you're after a stock replacement.

Molded carpet, however, fits the contours of the Mustang floorboard more or less exactly like the carpet

Ford installed in your car at the factory. There are various levels of quality here, and again, the carpet you choose depends upon what you want it for. Those people after a good usable rug, but one better than the flat standard rug described above, may want to go with a low cost molded set (they come in sets, for front and rear, of course). It's your decision. What we want to do is to describe the choices that you have on today's market.

MAKING "OEM" CARPET, 1964½-1973

Back in 1964 and 1965, and on through 1973, when suppliers made carpets on contract for Ford's Mustang, they started with a good heavy "jute-back". Jute is a glossy fiber chiefly used for sack, burlap,

and twine. For auto carpets, the jute-back is a coarse, heavy burlap fabric, which provides the initial backing to accept the carpet threads. Of course, this backing comes in various weights, but for the Mustang the heavy-weight jute-back was used. A special machine — with row after row of needles — inserts loops of thread into this backing. The thread used for the 1964½ through 1966 models was called "80/20", which is 80% rayon and 20% nylon. For the 1967 and up models, a heavy-duty 100% nylon was stock. At this point, the carpet is gray/white — what is called "greige" — and it is dyed next. Later, a "poly" backing is applied. Spread out on the back side of the jute-back, it goes through a series of heat and cool operations, so that the poly penetrates the carpet for a good slick finish, and locks in the loops of

72

thread for a permanent bond. Next, these rolls of carpet, maybe 100 or 500 yards long, are cut down to block size. Then, the carpet is placed in molds and reheated, causing the "poly" (which is short for polyethylene) to melt, and take on the molded shape which is the shape of your floorboard. Finally, the carpet goes through the trimming-finishing process. The heel/toe pads are sewn in place, the edges are "serged", holes are made for the headlight dimmer switches, gear shift levers, etc.

Of course, we no longer can buy original carpet from Ford, because the contracts with the original equipment suppliers are discontinued. These big suppliers are making carpet for the new models. But the Mustang market is so large that we have smaller supliers making carpet — but in various degrees of quality.

GETTING THE RIGHT MATERIALS

As we said, for 1964½ through 1966 the "loop pile" itself was made of "80/20", which is a combination yarn of 80% rayon and 20% nylon. About 1967, the major manufacturers started changing over to all nylon and Mustang carpets from 1967 through 1973 used nylon threads instead of 80/20. The change to all nylon came as improvements in nylon resulted in material which was longer wearing and more fade resistant than the old 80/20.

Today, replacement carpet for 1964½ to 1966 Mustangs is made in 80/20 and all nylon, and both are considered correct. The 1967 through 1973 carpets are remade from heavy weight nylon. But what if you try and save twenty to thirty dollars on your carpet purchase? Well, your new carpet will look much like stock; it will be molded, but you will be getting a cheaper, muck lighter weight material. When you buy carpet, you are buying by weight. And remember, after stepping on the carpet, pressing your feet on it, it will compact itself down, and the cheaper, lower weight nylon will look and even feel thinner!

The jute-back also comes in various weights, and any manufacturer could order one of their unfinished stocks with a cheaper backing, if he so desired. Okay for some buyers, but unacceptable if you want the proper carpet as per original specs.

GETTING THE RIGHT STYLE

We have a similar situation with toe/heel pads. For the first generation Mustang, there were many sizes of these toe/heel pads. For example, the

If you own a 1964½ Mustang, be sure to specify no toe pad.

convertible pad was different from the pad in the coupes and fastback (due to the extra bracing in the convertible along with the lower sides of the car, making for about two inches less width). If you own a 1964½, it is common knowledge that the carpet was changed in 1965-1966 when the familiar toe/heel pad was added. So today, the remanufacturer can either sew-in this pad, or leave it off. And these carpets are available either way. Also, the "trim-line" is different on the 1964½, with a vinyl sidewall along the edges, running up under the sill plate when installed in the car. Again, the remanufacturer can add this vinyl while the carpet is in the sewing stage — which is done today. So don't install a '65-type carpet in your '64½. Keep looking, and you'll find

that 1964½-type!

As another common example, suppose you own a 1965-1966 fastback. Then, the rear portion of the carpet must be trimmed specially to accommodate the rear seat armrest cutout.

You can see that you need to inspect your carpet for your particular model year/body style combination, and then buy a carpet to match it as closely as possible. We do suggest that, if your Mustang still has its OEM carpet, you keep it stored for future reference.

The hobby and business of owning and collecting Mustangs is constantly changing and growing, and we plan to keep you up to date in these pages. It is our job to supply you with the current facts, so you can make the right choices for your own purpose. What was it Jack Webb used to say on "Dragnet"? Just the facts ma'am"?

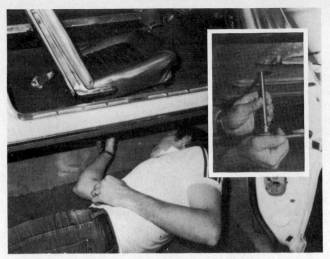

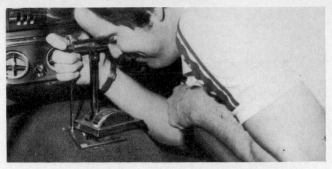

Remove the four plugs underneath each front bucket seat, on the underside of the floorpan. Then, using a ½" deep socket with extension, unscrew the four nuts that hold each seat in place.

IF YOU HAVE AUTOMATIC TRANSMISSION: With an allen wrench, loosen the allen head screw that secures the shifter to the handle. Then pull the shifter handle off its shaft. Next, unscrew the four screws that hold the shift indicator bezel to the transmission tunnel, and pull it over the top of the shaft. Underneath this bezel is a steel plate, also secured by four screws. Remove this plate the same way.

If you have a console: For "short" consoles (an accessory for air conditioned Mustangs), remove three screws from each side of the console. For "long" consoles (an accessory for non-air conditioned Mustangs), remove two screws from inside the console glove box. Starting with the back of the console, lift and remove.

Lift each bucket seat straight up, and out. Pick up the seat track spacers from the top of the carpet — one spacer for each seat stud, four for each bucket seat.

IF YOU HAVE AIR CONDITIONING: Disconnect the drain hose from the evaporator case. Then, reach underneath the rug, and unplug the hose from the floorboard.

Remove the rear seat back rest, then the rear seat cushion. The back rest pulls off by lifting it up, off a pair of hooks. Now it is easy to grab the back of the seat cushion, and pull it out.

Remove the "scuff" plates (secured by screws) that hold the carpet to the sides of the car. One screw is common with the front kick panels.

Remove the "kick" panels forward of the doors. They are secured by two screws, but one screw will already be removed, since it is common with the scuff plate.

Remove two screws — one on each side of the car — that secure the carpet to the inner trim panels, at the bottom, just behind the scuff plate.

Unscrew the seat belt bolts from the rear floorboard.

IF YOU HAVE AN AIR CONDITIONER: Adjust the set screw directly underneath the evaporator case, so that you can pull out the old carpet.

Remove the old carpet, pulling it over the headlight dimmer switch and the gearshift housing. Then pull out the floor pads and sweep the floorboard clear of debris.

NEW CARPET REPLACEMENT

Put the old floor pads back into place, and lay-in the new carpet, both sets — front and rear. Lay the carpet flat, positioning it over the transmission shifter housing and the headlight dimmer switch.

IF YOU HAVE AUTOMATIC TRANSMISSION: Replace the steel plate with the four retaining screws. Trim the carpet so that it fits like your original carpet. Now tighten the screws, and replace the transmission indicator bezel. Replace the shift handle and tighten the Allen head screw.

Using a sharp point — your Phillips head screwdriver works fine — punch holes for the seat belt bolts. Then, push the bolts through the carpet, and start the threads. Then tighten the bolts. Remember that the seat belt buckles go on the inside, and the plain straps to the outside.

Pop the rear seat cushion into place. Then rehang the rear seat back rest.

IF YOU HAVE AIR CONDITIONING: Cut a hole for the drain hose. Then replug it into the floorboard, and into the evaporator case.

IF YOU HAVE AIR CONDITIONING: Readjust the set screw directly underneath the evaporator case (arrow), so that it touches the new carpet.

Replace the two screws — one on each side of the car — that secure the carpet to the rear inner trim panels, at the bottom, just behind the scuff plate.

Replace the kick panels, forward of the doors. Secure them with one screw each, and keep the other screw ready for its common use with the scuff plate.

Replace the scuff plates that secure the carpet to the sides of the car.

IF YOU HAVE A CONSOLE: Position the console on the transmission shift tunnel, setting the front end in place first. Secure the "short" console with its three screws on each side. Secure the "long" console with its two screws from inside the console glove box.

Punch holes through the carpet for the bucket seat studs. Then position each seat over the four holes in the floorboard, and push the studs through the bottom. Take the seat track spacers and slip them under each corner.

Using a ½" deep socket with extension, screw-in the nuts that hold each seat in place. (Be sure not to overtighten!) Replace the four plugs for each front bucket seat, on the underside of the floorpan.

Wow, what a difference new carpet makes! Now my '66 coupe even smells like new! And what is so satisfying is that I did the whole "R&R" (remove and replace) myself.

The entire job takes four to six hours, and can be done by one person. In fact, our advice is to install the rug yourself, if you are physically able. You'll get to know your Mustang better, you'll get a good feeling of a job well done, and you'll save the labor of about $20 per hour!

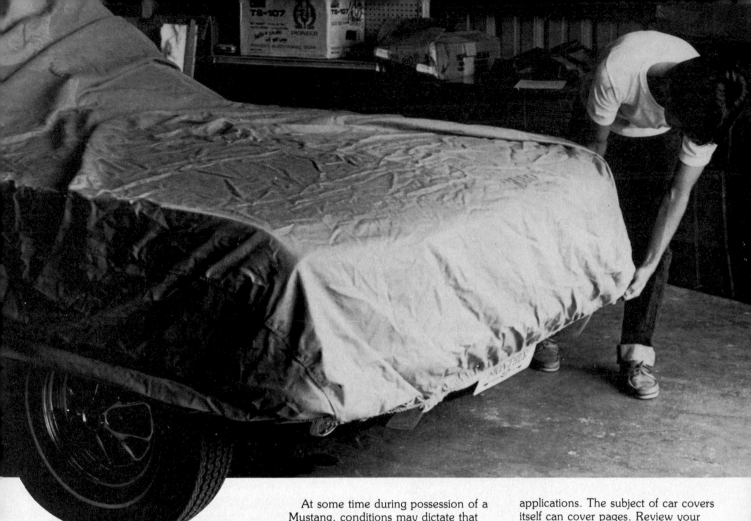

How To
PREPARE YOUR MUSTANG FOR STORAGE

by Jerry Ostalecki

Removing the rubber floor mats will allow the carpet to ventilate during the storage period.

At some time during possession of a Mustang, conditions may dictate that you "store" your pride and joy. Whether it's severe winter weather or the decision of the grand jury that forces your pony into storage, proper preparation can eliminate any likelihood of ill effects later on.

First and foremost, consideration should be given to the duration of storage. The length of storage has a profound effect on the amount of preparation needed. Storage duration can be divided into two categories: long term or short term. Any period of inactivity over nine months would be considered long term. Shorter durations, including winter storage, fall into the short term category. We will examine the points to be considered for both long and short term storage.

SHORT TERM STORAGE

First, check the available storage area. At one end of the scale is the gigantic plastic baggie filled with your pony and inert gas, and on the other end is the spot in the field out back where the cows don't go. If conditions dictate the field as the only available location, all is not lost. A quality car cover will provide some protection from the elements. I feel that a car cover is an important part of any storage, inside or out, because it helps prevent airborne pollutants from settling on the paint. Covers are available in various weaves for different

applications. The subject of car covers itself can cover pages. Review your situation and contact one of the suppliers found in Mustang Monthly for their recommendations.

The ideal storage area is a garage or similar structure. But, in most cases, even garages will need some type of preparation prior to the storage period. Make certain your pony will not sit under a leaky spot in the roof. Clear out an area where you won't be forced to move the car everytime you need something from the area. Once your spot is staked out, spread some 4 mil plastic on the floor. The plastic should extend about one foot beyond the car, but not so far as to be a hazard when walking in the area. The plastic is important because it prevents floor moisture from rising and settling on the undercarriage. This moisture can make a mess of the entire undercarriage in short order.

With a safe spot located and plastic in place, preparation of the Mustang is the next order of business. The exterior should be washed thoroughly to remove any road film. If the car is due for wax, now is the time to apply it. After spiffing up the exterior, it's time to move into the interior. Remove the floor mats to allow the carpet to ventilate and scrub the entire passenger compartment.

Next area of attention is under the hood. If you need a tune up after a season of driving, this would be the best

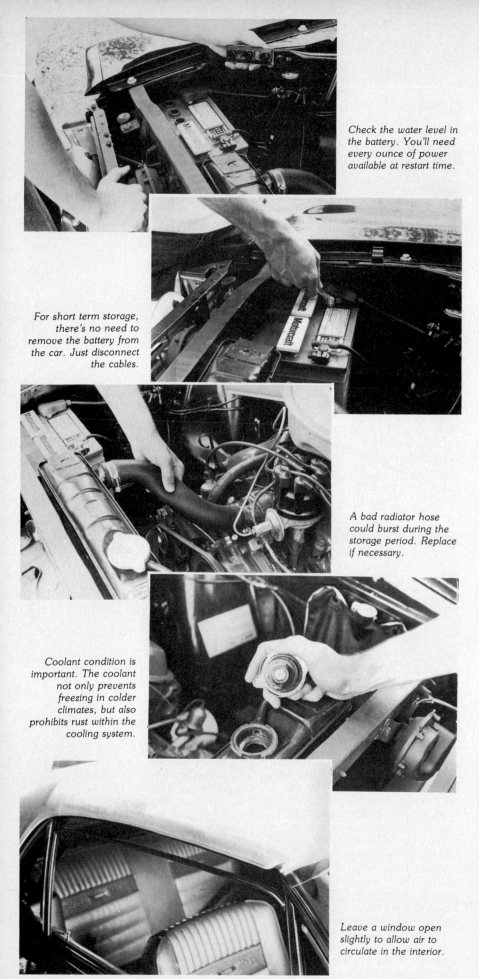

Check the water level in the battery. You'll need every ounce of power available at restart time.

For short term storage, there's no need to remove the battery from the car. Just disconnect the cables.

A bad radiator hose could burst during the storage period. Replace if necessary.

Coolant condition is important. The coolant not only prevents freezing in colder climates, but also prohibits rust within the cooling system.

Leave a window open slightly to allow air to circulate in the interior.

time for you to have it done. Check all belts for cracks and fraying. If your coolant is an unmentionable color, a flush and fill would be in order. Use a quality antifreeze solution mixed in proper portion, as called for on the container, to prevent both coolant freezing and rust formation. Also keep in mind that any marginal radiator or heater hose may burst, dumping that solution on the ground for you. A complete examination of all hoses is a must item. Finally, change the oil and filter.

Check the battery fluid level and search for any sign of terminal corrosion. A minute speck today can grow to power robbing proportions before you know it. Inspect the cables for splits in the insulation or cracks in the clamp. Replace if necessary. When you start the engine after the period of storage, you will need all the power your battery can supply.

The gas tank should be filled to ½ to ¾ capacity to reduce the possibility of condensation. In addition, the last tank prior to storage should be treated with dry gas to remove any present condensation in the system. Don't forget to add an antifreeze solution to the windshield washer fluid if the temperature will dip below freezing. Bring tire pressure up to specification for the storage period.

With everything in top-notch condition, pull the car into it's storage area. Don't forget the plastic floor covering. Once in position, remove the negative or positive cable from the battery post. You may want to remove the battery from the car, but doing so brings up a whole new set of problems. With it removed, you must find a safe spot to store it. I have found it simpler to leave the battery in place.

Leave one window open slightly to permit air to circulate in the interior and prevent that musty odor. But don't open it far enough to permit rodents to take up residence inside your pony.

With everything squared away, place the cover over the car. Don't forget to stow the keys where you can find them when the storage period ends.

I had the opportunity to discuss automobile storage with Randy Mason, Associate Curator of the Transportation Collection at the Henry Ford Museum in Dearborn. Mr. Mason advises not to completely store a car, but during the period of inactivity, drive the car around the block occasionally. Even when weather is the reason for storage, a period of favorable conditions may permit that essential 15 minute cruise. Running the engine is fine during storage, but driving a short distance will lubricate the transmission and keep the brakes and other components in good condition.

If that break in weather fails to appear, and you can't back the car out for that short trip, you should at least run the engine at fast idle for 45 minutes. According to Mr. Mason, fast idle would be in the area of 2,000 RPM.

LONG TERM STORAGE

Preparing your Mustang for a long period of inactivity requires more mechanical preparation than short term.

Keep in mind that if you will be able to drive your car periodically for short distances during the storage period, the long term preparation steps will not be necessary. These steps should be performed only if you plan to store the car without driving it at all during the storage period.

Long term storage preparation begins with the steps found in the previous short term section. Then, after completing that portion, the brake system should be completely flushed and refilled with fresh fluid. Brake fluid has the ability to absorb moisture, and flushing and renewing the fluid will remove any moisture presently in the system. Fresh fluid will reduce the chance of brake line corrosion. (Silicone brake fluid will not be discussed here — arm yourself with facts before investing in silicone fluid.) When purchasing brake fluid for your garage, keep in mind that an open container will also absorb moisture. When I purchase brake fluid for maintaining my fleet, I buy a couple of smaller size cans rather than the monster size. This way I only open one small can at a time and expose a minimum of fluid to possible contamination. When the time comes to open the other can, it is factory fresh.

After miles of use, automatic transmission fluid may also become contaminated. Leaving the old fluid in the transmission during the storage period may result in damage to internal components. A complete change of fluid would be in order for a long term storage period. Don't forget to drain the torque converter when changing the fluid. For the shift-it-yourself crowd, check the fluid level in manual transmission Mustangs.

After completing this portion of preparation, the car should be moved to the storage site. The following procedures will render the car unmovable under its own power.

With the motor running at fast idle and the air cleaner removed, pour motor oil into the carburetor. Pour the oil quickly enough to permit the engine to run for a short period, then stall. The oil will coat the pistons and valves

Cover the dash pad and other vinyl interior parts with a quality protectant, such as "Armour-All" or "Sun-Of-A-Gun" to prevent drying out or possible rot.

A thorough cleaning of the interior will eliminate pollutants.

preventing corrosion during the storage period. Some oil will also find its way into the exhaust system which will help prevent internal rusting of the pipes.

Next, remove the valve covers and back off the rocker arms. This will remove any strain placed on the valve springs. With nonadjustable rocker arm assemblies, it will be necessary to remove the rocker arm shaft to insure that all valves are seated.

Any gasoline left in the fuel system can turn into a varnish-type sludge, causing problems later when the Mustang is restarted. The fuel tank should be drained of any remaining fuel. Likewise, the fuel pump should be free of fuel. It may also be necessary to remove the carb to drain any remaining fuel from the float bowl.

The car can be placed on jack stands if you desire. The car should be supported by the suspension as opposed to letting the wheels and suspension hang extended. One advantage of placing the car on stands is that the wheel bearings are not supporting the car. It is possible that, after a period of time, a flat spot may develop on the roller or ball of the bearings, leading to premature failure when the pony is put back on the road.

For long term storage, remove the battery and cables. Leaving the battery in the car for long term storage serves no purpose. Removing the cables will prevent any corrosion from spreading to other body panels and causing damage.

With the car supported by jack

stands, the wheels and tires can be removed if you desire. Store them away from any electrical appliances — the ozone produced by electrical appliances will age and destroy tires. Prior to storage, the tires should receive a good scrubbing and an application of a protectant such as "Armour All" or STP "Son of a Gun". Bring inflation up to max pressure as recommended on the side wall. This will help retain the rim seal.

The steering linkages should receive fresh grease for the storage period. Don't forget to lubricate the universal joints if the drive shaft is equipped with fittings. Check the level of lubricant in the differential.

A good coat of protectant on the tires will prevent rot during the storage period.

ON THE ROAD AGAIN

When the time arrives to reactivate the pony after its dormant period, certain steps will make a smoother transition. First, install fresh spark plugs and check the condition of the points. Inspect all underhood components. Install a fresh battery for that needed spark. Adjusting the valves readies the motor for action.

The condition of the grease in the front wheel bearings should be checked before putting the pony on the road. Depending on the duration of storage, the grease may have dried out. Driving a car with dried out bearings would destroy them in no time. A fresh shot of lubricant to the suspension components will prepare that area for service.

The brake fluid should be flushed and renewed. This will remove any moisture that may have found it's way into the brake system during storage. A check of brake component condition should also be performed prior to service.

Replace any items removed for the storage term.

Before operating the awakened beauty on the highway, a slow check-out cruise would be in order. Permit those internal parts to become reacquainted before getting in the fast lane.

Having followed all the short term and long term preparation recommendations, your pony should be able to handle the storage period with a minimum of problems. Many of the preparations recommended fall under the category of good maintenance. The effort put into storage preparation will be rewarded with future trouble free operation. With a little attention to the right areas, any possibility of ill effects from inactivity can be removed.

How To
DETAIL YOUR MUSTANG FOR SHOW

by Donald Farr

Springtime means showtime, and Mustang clubs all over the U.S. and Canada are gearing up for the warm weather months ahead. Just look at our bulging "Coming Events" page this month. Mustang owners, too, are preparing for the shows; many spent the past several months in their garages — at least the ones with heaters — shining up this, repainting that, and even undertaking full frame-up restorations. A lot of frozen sweat fell on concrete floors this past winter, just for the sake of adding a few more trophies to the mantle-piece.

Whether you rebuilt your Mustang last winter, or lounged around watching football, this article will assist you in preparing your Mustang for show competition. In fact, even if you don't plan to enter any shows, the information here will help you clean your Mustang for fun driving in the months ahead.

TYPE OF JUDGING

The amount of show cleaning and preparation will depend on the type of judging used at the particular shows you attend. Less time and effort is required for the "Popular Choice" judging method where the show participants vote for their favorite cars. No need to spend several dirty hours cleaning and detailing the undercarriage — most show participants check only the exterior, interior, and engine compartment. Of course, there's nothing wrong with detailing the underside, if you've got the time and patience, but most show attendees won't even bother to crawl down on their knees to look.

Judged Mustang shows, on the other hand, require meticulous cleaning and detailing, including the undercarriage — Mustang show judges don't mind crawling around on their hands and knees to look for rust and dirt on your floorpan. Even if your Mustang has a big rusty spot on the rear quarter, at least the rust should be clean. As expected, the big-buck restorations hold an advantage over the everyday street Mustangs (although many full-fledge restorations lose points for being over restored) because they don't contend with mud, rain, and road film on an everyday basis. However, just last year, the Mustang Club of America injected a special street driven class for owners of everyday Mustangs.

Except for modified classes, originality plays an important role in Mustang show judging. A bevy of minor infractions — an incorrect screw, a non-original radio, yellow spark plug wires — can knock your Mustang right out of trophy contention. We won't dive into the originality aspect here; pick up a copy of the Mustang Club of America's Judging Rules (for $1.50, from MCA Accessories, c/o Frank White, 349 Roberts Road, Marietta, Georgia 30066) since most U.S. and Canadian Mustang clubs, even those not sanctioned by the MCA, abide by their point system. The rule book won't tell you exactly what parts are correct for your particular Mustang — no book does, except maybe the Ford Master Parts Catalog — but it will steer you in the right direction.

SPRING CLEANING

The Mustang Club of America's point system deducts a maximum of 250 points for originality, but it also adds up to 250 points for cleanliness, condition, and quality of workmanship. To lose all

At judged concours shows, your Mustang should be meticulously clean, or the judges will start clipping points from your total score.

Many Mustang show participants wait until the morning of the show to begin their preparations. Even if you clean your Mustang early, you'll need to tidy up odds and ends once you park in the show area.

250 originality points you'd have to enter a Camaro, so a clean, neat Mustang stands a better chance of bringing home a trophy.

If you've got the time and motivation, you can tidy up sections of your Mustang over a week-end. Our June, 1981, issue details how to clean your engine compartment, and, in our July, 1981, issue, a similar article, "How To Make Your Inferior Interior Superior", outlines an interior restoration. Both projects can be performed on a budget basis, although the interior redo could become expensive if you need new upholstery and carpet.

Basic show preparations can be performed during the week-end and week nights before the show, unless your Mustang is driven everyday. In fact, many Mustang owners wait until the morning of the show to begin their

cleaning; there's nothing like climbing out of your warm bed and stepping out into the cool morning air with a water-filled trash can and a box full of rags and Windex. Depending on your particular Mustang and whether or not you drive it everyday, most Mustangs can be properly prepared for showing within a couple of hours. Major cleaning and touch-ups, such as steam cleaning and/or repainting the engine, should be done at least several days in advance, then you can complete the final detailing at the show site.

PRELIMINARY CLEANING

During the weeks and days prior to show date, tackle any time-consuming cleaning or touch-up chores. Head for the nearest steam cleaner or 50¢ spray car wash for an engine and undercarriage clean-up. Cover the

distributor and carburetor with plastic (a sandwich wrap secured with rubber bands works well), coat heavy grease accumulations with Gunk degreaser, wait a few minutes for the Gunk to soak in, then hose off with the steam cleaner or pressurized car wash. Unless you're planning to completely repaint the engine and engine compartment, try to keep the main force of the water away from painted areas — the force will often peel the paint. Be sure to hit inside the wheelwells and the front suspension, since most show judges inspect those areas with a fine tooth comb. Don't forget the underside of the hood, and shoot some water through the radiator from the engine side to force out accumulated bugs and trash.

GETTING NITTY-GRITTY

Before diving into your Mustang head first, stand back and outline your plan of attack. This business of spring cleaning is just as tiring mentally as it is physically, so you need to prepare your mind for the task ahead. It's a boring job that requires patience and willingness. Divide the Mustang into 5 sections — interior, exterior, engine compartment, undercarriage, and trunk — and work on each area separately, finishing one before starting another.

UNDERCARRIAGE

Because it's the dirtiest and least satisfying area to clean (not to mention the most difficult to reach!), the undercarriage is the most logical area to begin with — just to get the chore behind you! As mentioned earlier, the amount of undercarriage preparation will depend on the show judging; if it's popular choice, you may want to eliminate any additional cleaning under the car. But if concours judging is planned, a couple of extra hours underneath could spell the difference between first and second — or third or fourth — place.

Start by inspecting the front suspension. The steam cleaning should have eliminated most of the heavy grease, but some will remain, so wipe it off (or scrape it off if you must) with an old rag soaked with a degreaser or cleaner. Pay particular attention to highly visible parts like the strut bars, steering linkage, and sway bar. And while you're under there, wipe off the oil pan.

A little chassis black touch-up paint will make the front suspension look like new, but be careful — the judges will penalize for overspray. Try to avoid originally unpainted parts — rubber bushings, spacers, etc. If you've got plenty of time, you can even mask unpainted areas with masking tape and newspaper.

Ideally, the exhaust system should be

unpainted and unrusted, but that's an unobtainable goal for most of us. So, even though it's unoriginal, you may fare better by painting the exhaust with high temperature black paint. Clean paint looks better than rust anytime.

The rear suspension can be cleaned with a cleaner-soaked cloth. Wipe all painted surfaces, including the springs, rear end housing, shocks, and frame. The natural finish gas tank can be cleaned with fine steel wool and aluminum polish.

If you drive your Mustang everyday, don't go overboard cleaning the undercarriage — one good, messy rainfall will ruin hours of cleaning.

ENGINE COMPARTMENT

Here's where you *can* go overboard. Everybody admires a clean, neat, shiny engine compartment, including Mustang show judges. The preliminary steam cleaning or spray wash should have left you with a fairly clean engine and compartment, except for a few water spots and lingering dirt. Some all-purpose cleaner (like 409 or Fantastik) on a clean rag will remove these traces.

Many show competitors overlook the underside of the hood. A little elbow grease and some pre-wax cleaner can make the hood underside look as good as the car's exterior. Radiators are another often forgotten area — bugs and weeds hanging from the fins ruin an otherwise clean radiator. With patience and a pair of household tweezers, you can pick the radiator fins clean.

Touch-up paint goes a long way toward extra points in the cleanliness category. You can touch-up large areas by aiming the spray can carefully. Smaller scratches and chips can be filled in with a modeler's brush. Don't overlook bolt heads. Any overspray or drips can be quickly wiped away with a lacquer thinner-soaked cloth.

Good engine chrome cleans easily with a glass cleaner like Windex or Glass-Plus. In fact, if you've never tried a glass cleaner on chrome, you'll be surprised by the shine. Don't use polish unless the chrome is pitted or corroded; chrome polishes contain abrasives that will scratch good, slick chrome.

Aluminum and natural metal parts can be cleaned with the aluminum cleaners found at your local automotive parts store. Use fine steel wool on tubular gas lines.

While you're under the hood, check the condition of hoses, belts, clamps, and other general maintenance items. Frayed belts and bulging hoses detract points according to the Mustang Club of America guidelines, not to mention thrown belts and busted hoses leaving you stranded on the roadside. I remember one fellow who spent most of a week-end cleaning and detailing his

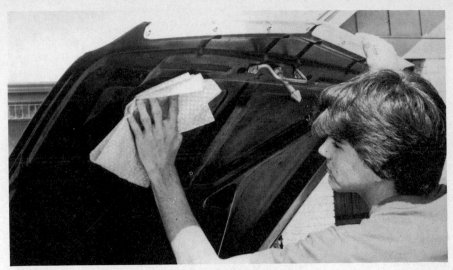

Don't forget to clean under the hood. A little pre-wax cleaner and some elbow grease will usually add new shine to old, dull paint.

Using a modeler's brush (available at most art supply stores) and a paint can cap, dab touch-up paint into chips and scratches on the engine. This method also works well for touching up bolt heads.

Here's an example of a neat, clean, well-kept engine and engine compartment.

Mustang for a show, only to have a busted radiator hose spray geen antifreeze all over his sparkling engine as he drove into the show parking area.

Wiring appearance is critical. Paint overspray and age-old grease cleans off easily enough with lacquer thinner. Use black electrical tape to rewrap loose wires.

Finally, wipe all rubber and plastic surfaces with a protectant like Armor-All, Sun-Of-A-Gun, etc.

TRUNK

In terms of importance at popular choice shows, the trunk compartment rates a 4 — behind the exterior, interior, and engine compartment, but ahead of the undercarriage. However, at judged concours shows, the points deducted from the trunk count just as much as those taken from the exterior paint. So your trunk needs to be as clean and neat as possible.

Start by emptying the trunk contents — spare tire, jack, trunk mat, tool box, beach blanket, old beer cans, etc. Vacuum the entire trunk interior, especially around the gas tank lip where chunks of rust and chipped paint usually collect. Fantastik or 409 can be used to effectively clean the painted surfaces — inner fenders, trunk lid hinges, latch, etc. Lay the trunk mat flat on the ground or work bench, then vacuum thoroughly before scrubbing with a good general purpose cleaner and brush. You can't restore an old well-used mat to like-new condition — short of buying a new one — but you can make the old mat as clean as possible.

Don't forget to clean under the trunk lid. A pre-wax cleaner will remove old grease and grime, and possibly restore some of the long-lost shine. Coat the rubber gasket with Armor-All.

With the spare on the ground, scrub the tire with one of the many tire cleaners currently available — most seem to work very well. Don't overlook the tread because much of it shows with the spare lying in the trunk. Clean the spare's rim with a cleaner. Coat the tire with Armor-All for that like-new shine.

Carefully replace the trunk mat, positioning it as neatly as possible. Then reinstall the spare tire, jack, and jack handle in their proper positions.

INTERIOR

Because of their complexity, Mustang interiors are difficult to clean; but, for the same reason, they are difficult to judge. So, if you're short on time, concentrate on the obvious items — the seats, door panels, crash pad, console, carpet, and all chrome. Interior appearance is especially important in a convertible if the cars are judged with the tops down; sunlight will reveal every scratch and flaw.

This trunk compartment appears extremely clean, but the trunk mat could use some additional straightening. Neatness counts, too.

Begin inside by cleaning the upholstery. Fantastik is fantastic at removing dirt, but you'll need a more potent cleaner like Genie Clean to get at the oxidized portion of the vinyl. Use a stiff-bristled toothbrush to scrub woven vinyl seat inserts and deep grain vinyl. Don't overlook the back seats, or even the seat backs. Door panels and plastic rear quarter trim also clean up well with Fantastik.

Clean all the interior glass and chrome with Windex, Glass-Plus or other suitable glass cleaner. Don't forget the rear view mirror or plasti-chrome items like instrument knobs or door panel trim.

Remove the floor mats and lay them flat on the ground or work bench. Spray on a generous amount of Fantastik or tire cleaner, then scrub with a course brush. Rinse with water and hang out to dry. Later, you can coat the mats with Armor-All.

While the floor mats are out, vacuum the carpet thoroughly, reaching under and around the front seats.

Lastly, coat the wonder-lotion Armor-All (or, in all fairness, one of the other protectants on the market) on all interior vinyl and rubber, including the crash pad. Not only will the parts shine like new, but the protectant will prevent the sun's rays from discoloring (or cracking, in the case of the crash pad) your upholstery.

EXTERIOR

Assuming that your Mustang's paint is fairly good, you'll probably need only a wash and wax, and maybe even a pre-wax if the paint is oxidized. Any major paint repairs or reconditioning (ranging from a buff to repainting) should be performed well in advance.

Every individual develops his or her own method of car washing, and one is just as good as another. Be sure to hose off the car with plain water first to rinse away any sand or grit that could scratch your car's finish. Then use a good detergent and a sponge or rag to clean road film and dirt. Many car

washing solutions are available at your local automotive parts store, so we can't list them all. Some are designed for freshly waxed cars — they won't strip away any wax — so read the label. The stronger soaps are better if you plan to wax your car, but the milder solutions are best if you've recently waxed. Wipe all areas of the car carefully — you'd be surprised at the number of Mustangs that show up with big dirt blotches on the door; the dirt is difficult to see when the car is wet. Wash sections of the car, then rinse — especially in the hot sun — because dried soap can cause spots.

Immediately after washing, dry the Mustang with a towel (or several towels), chamois, or The Absorber to prevent any water spotting.

Clean the tires with one of the many available tire cleaners. Rinse off the tire, squirt on the cleaner, scrub with a stiff brush (especially white walls and letters), and rinse off.

If your Mustang has been waxed several times, you may want to use a pre-wax cleaner to remove the old wax build-up. These are usually harder to locate since many waxes today include a built-in cleaner. Some familiar names are Prep-Sol, Pre-Cleano, Meguiar's, and The Treatment. The pre-wax cleaners can also be used to remove tar from the rocker panels and fenders.

Before waxing, touch-up any stone chips and/or scratches with a can of touch-up paint and a modeler's brush. Go around the entire car, paying particular attention to the rocker panels, rear quarters, and doors.

Again, we can't begin to name all the wax products on the market today, so use your personal favorite. Some contain abrasives (usually called "one step" wax cleaners), so we don't recommend them for good, slick paint jobs — they can scratch. However, if your Mustang's paint is faded, the cleaner/waxes can work to your advantage. For slick finishes, use a pure wax, or one of the cleaner/waxes designed for show cars (like Meguiar's Car Cleaner-Wax). Use an old

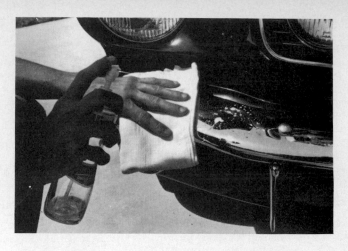

Rubber floor mats clean easily enough with a general purpose cleaner (like Fantastik or 409) and a stiff brush. Or you can use one of the many tire cleaners found at the local automotive parts store. After drying, coat with Armor-All.

Glass cleaners work well on chrome, too. In fact, if your chrome is like new, we recommend Windex or a similar cleaner over chrome polish.

One of the best new cleaning products on the market today is Genie Clean, a vinyl and leather cleaner that actually reconditions the vinyl. Most cleaners only remove the top dirt, but Genie Clean takes off many years of vinyl oxidation.

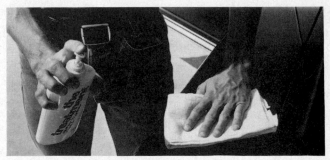

Tires can be scrubbed with a good whitewall tire cleaner, then coated to a brilliant shine with Armor-All. Windex or other suitable glass cleaner works wonders on chrome wheels.

The Treatment's Spray and Glow — if you can find it — is an excellent at-the-show cleaner and dust remover.

toothbrush to remove left-over wax from seams and stripe edges.

Clean all glass and chrome with a glass cleaner. Dulled chrome can be reconditioned some with a chrome polish, but don't expect miracles if the chrome is pitted. A quick buff with rubbing compound will help, too, but the only sure cure for pitted chrome is replacement or rechroming. Steel wool will also work wonders on slightly oxidized chrome. Don't forget the back-up lights, taillight trim, and chrome exhaust tips.

Finally, coat all exterior rubber, especially the tires, with Armor-All, although you may want to wait until you reach the show site.

AT THE SHOW

Be prepared for anything. If a sudden thunderstorm catches you en route to the show, you'll need to wash the car

all over again, so take along a bucket, soap, sponge, and all other materials. Even if it doesn't rain, you'll need to rinse off accumulated road film. Just fill a bucket (or a motel trash can) with water, wipe the car with a soaking-wet towel, then dry. Invest in a portable vacuum cleaner — they usually operate through the cigarette lighter — so you can clean out any sand or gravel picked up along the way.

Raise the hood and trunk, and wipe off accumulated dust with a treated dust cloth. If you've got the time, inspect the undercarriage, too.

One of The Treatment products, Spray and Glow, is an especially handy item to have around — if you can find it. Spray and Glow picks up dust and dirt like a magnet — sort of a funiture cleaner for cars — and even adds more shine to the wax. It's usually found at custom car shows.

The rest of the procedure is pretty much standard — wipe off the chrome, Armor-All the upholstery and tires again (including the tread), polish any aluminum, etc. Just remember to be thorough, stepping back occasionally to take a look to see what needs more attention.

When you're done, you can stroll through the show area checking out the competition (you may return quickly to your Mustang for more cleaning!). Just before the judges reach your car, give it one last wipe with a treated dust cloth.

Whether you win a trophy or not, you can stand back and admire your clean, neat Mustang. Driving it home later will be a fun experience — the surrounding interior will be shiny clean and other drivers on the road will gaze at your car, wondering how you keep your Mustang so new looking. They'll never know.

How To
PHOTOGRAPH YOUR MUSTANG

by Jerry Heasley

Photography is an immense subject! We could make this "how to" article an easy fifty pages long, and even then it would barely scratch the surface! So what we want to do here is to lay down some specific guidelines on how to photograph your Mustang. We'll include details on the different types of cameras and films (and which ones we prefer), and then we'll get into "competition", a term that separates a "snapshot" from a real "photograph". However, we'll leave most of the "brain-work — getting the right exposure, setting the camera controls, loading the film, and other less salient details — to you and your camera's instruction book. At least for now. But we think you'll be surprised at the polished, professional-looking pictures you'll get using the facts in this article.

At least for now. But we think you'll be surprised at the polished, professional-looking pictures you'll get using the facts in this article.

CAMERAS

You may have one of dozens of the different types of cameras on the market today, from a single-lens reflex to a twin-lens reflex, from a miniature camera to a big view camera. But for simplification, we'll divide cameras into three major categories, according to the size of the film they use. We are interested in a quality reproduction of your black and white print, or of your color slide. Any of the following types of cameras will work, but with certain pluses and minuses as follows:

CAMERAS USING "110" FILM:
These are the so-called "pocket" cameras. A popular example is the Kodak "Instamatic". We have used a few pictures taken with 110's, when the images are very sharp, but these cameras have several major disadvantages. Their biggest drawback is the very small size of the film, which means the quality of the print is decreased as the size of the print is increased. Another minus is that most "110" cameras have a fixed focus, a fixed aperture, and a fixed shutter speed. They are set on manufacture, so that everything is in focus from about six feet to infinity. You can see then, that it would be impossible to photograph details within six feet, and get that sharp image.

In the last couple years, Pentax has

85

come out with a 110 camera that has adjustable settings, which would correct many of the above problems, but you are still stuck with the very small film size. Of course, that's the main idea of a 110 — to carry a small camera that will fit in your pocket.

Overall, then, we can use some of the really sharp 110 pictures for our "Reader's Album", and they're fine for your personal collection. But they are hard to use for cases where we enlarge the negative or slide to say a half-page or more.

CAMERAS USING 35MM FILM: This format is ideal for "Mustang Monthly"! No matter what type of 35mm camera that you own, if you can get the focus, the exposure, and the composition on target, using the right film, you will have excellent pictures for these pages — and for your own personal use as well. Of course, 35mm cameras — Nikon, Minolta, Pentax, Olympus, Canon — have adjustable settings for focus, aperture, and shutter speed. The size of the 35mm film is still relatively small, but it is excellent for enlargements up to 8x10, and even larger, with good quality reproduction — check out this month's cover!

Use an old 35mm or a new 35mm, a cheap one or an expensive one. We are interested in the results!

CAMERAS USING 120 FILM: A wide variety of cameras use this type of film, from one of the old "Brownies" from the 1950's, to one of the advanced "single lens reflex" Hasselblad's of today. Of course, like the 110, the old Brownie had no provision for adjustment, which could mean a picture that is not sharp enough for use in these pages. But when the image is crisp and the composition is pleasing, even with one of these very cheap cameras you will have that excellent medium size format! A camera like the Hasselblad "ELM", on the other price end of the 120 scale, has practically unlimited potential; it was the camera that the astronauts took to the moon. Of course, it costs a couple thousand dollars, and then you can spend that much again for a wide angle lens!

The major advantage of cameras using 120 film is the generous size of the negative (or slide) — many times larger than the 35mm, which means excellent, professional reproduction capability. For example, the "ELM" is a "2¼ by 2¼" inch format, used by many top professional photographers.

You can see then, that pictures from 120 cameras are welcomed to "Mustang Monthly", when the images are sharp and clear, and the composition is right.

FILM

What about film? What kind should you shoot? Generally, use the film with the lowest "ASA" rating for the

Here's why we prefer black and white prints over color. This 1966 convertible photo is reproduced from an original black and white. Notice the sharpness and clarity in the reproduction...

...when compared to this original color print. The red GT fastback is beautiful in color, but when converted to a black and white halftone (for reproduction) the car becomes nearly black, losing much detail. Notice how the GT stripes disappear.

available light conditions. As you know, the higher the ASA number, the greater its sensitivity to light, which means it takes less exposure to produce an image. However, a higher ASA number also means an increase in the "grain", a decrease in contrast, and often a decrease in image sharpness. A lower ASA number generally means precisely the opposite — less sensitivity to light, which means it takes a greater exposure to produce an image, but the final picture will have greater detail sharpness.

BLACK AND WHITE FILM: For daylight shots, we like Kodak "Plus X", which has an ASA rating of 125. For even finer detail, when you have plenty of light for your particular camera, you might even go with "Panatomic X", which has an ASA number of 32. If you are shooting 120 film, however, even "Tri-X", which has an ASA number of 400, is okay — the negative is already so large that you don't have to be as concerned about grain in the enlargements. If you are using a 110 camera, however, you should now see that one good way to partially get around the smaller negative size is to shoot with the lowest speed film possible for the lighting situation.

COLOR FILM: At "Mustang Monthly" we need slides "transparencies), rather than color prints and color negatives (although color prints are okay). But for reasons of "color separation" in the printing process, it is much more convenient for a magazine to have slides, rather than negatives. Slides are "positives", or the reverse of "negatives".

For daylight shooting, use

Kodachrome 64 (ASA = 64), or Kodachrome 25 (ASA = 25), which is an even finer grain positive. However, if you are using 120 film, Kodachrome is unavailable, and you will have to buy another slide film. We suggest Ektachrome 200 or Ektachrome 400. Of course, as always, under low light situations with your 35mm, you can also go to a higher speed slide film — Ektachrome 200 or Ektachrome 400.

PROCESSING YOUR FILM: For black and white prints, it's best to go to a professional lab. A key point is that you don't have to print every negative; that can prove very costly. The number one alternative is to order a "contact" sheet, which is an 8½x11 inch print of a whole roll of negatives, arranged side by side. These "proof sheets" are handy to choose pictures from for custom printing. You can also have contact prints made for your own personal color negatives, then pick out which shots you want, and have them printed for your own personal album. It will save lots of dollars, saving you from printing pictures that you discover less than desirable on the contact.

With slide film, processing is a different story. No printing is involved since the positive film itself is the image. The smaller labs are not set up to handle Kodachrome, which is a very involved, expensive process. Kodak has a fine reputation for developing slides, or you may have good luck with another large processing firm. Practically every small lab can do Ektachrome, however. In fact, many amateurs learn to do this developing at their kitchen sink.

PHOTOGRAPHING YOUR MUSTANG

Now for the interesting part — composition. You have the right film, and the right camera for the job, and you know how to use them. What now?

First, whenever possible, have a spot picked out BEFORE you jump in your Mustang and start cruising around, looking for a place to shoot. Choose a spot with an uncluttered background, and above all make sure it has plenty of available light to illuminate the car. Position your Mustang so that the light comes over your shoulder, and onto your car. You can shoot with the sun high in the sky, or low. However, a bright overhead sun will wash out the contours and details of your Mustang. So choose a more flattering lower sun angle (morning or later afternoon), which will better reveal the shapes on the surface of your Ford.

As far as backgrounds, you can assure good composition if you keep it simple. An example is open countryside, with earth and sky. Tom Senter, editor of POPULAR HOT RODDING, recently showed me some transparencies of a performance car at Bonneville — nothing but the salt flats, glorious sky, and machine. What a spectacular series of photos!

If you choose a building for a backdrop, it's a good idea to utilize a part of the architecture, rather than to try and include the whole structure in the background (unless the building is off in the distance). Why? Well, as an example, I recently saw a picture of an old car set against a turn-of-the-century three story house; but the house took up over three-fourths of the picture. So what do you want, a picture of a house, or a picture of your car? It's your choice. But remember that for these pages, we want to see your Mustang, not the Taj Mahal.

The same reasoning goes for other backgrounds. We don't want a picture of the Grand Canyon with your Mustang a tiny speck on the landscape. Save those shots for "travel log" magazines. Yes, do look for pretty and interesting backgrounds, but make your Mustang the center of attention!

Also, make sure backgrounds are free of telephone poles, TV antennas, and such, which in a two-dimensional picture can appear to be growing out of the top of the car.

For photo sessions with your Mustang, keep other vehicles out of the field of view (especially Chevrolets!).

In cases where you cannot move a particular Mustang to improve background composition (such as at a car show), you can use a small depth of field "f" number to blur-out undesirable background color.

Watch out for shadows from trees, buildings, poles, and other tall objects. Also, with the sun coming directly from the side, the front end loses detail in the shadow.

This is more like it! Just by moving the car ahead a few feet and adjusting the angle, we eliminated the unsightly shadows and aimed more sunlight onto the front end.

The "ant in a shoebox" picture. The Mustang is the hero, not the house, so move in and fill your camera's frame with beautiful, classic Mustang.

Late afternoon or early morning sun causes long shadows. Spectators, and even yourself, can get into a photograph and onto the car via shadows.

If your Mustang is white, or light-colored, use a contrasting darker background so that the outline of your vehicle is vivid, and shows up to the reader. If the car is darker, perhaps a lighter-colored background will better outline the whole exterior. We get too many pictures with dark on dark, and light on light. Follow the outline of the body and make sure it does not disappear into the background. A common mistake is a white Mustang silhouetted against a light sky — the top just disappears! So use your common sense with lights and colors, searching for contrasts to outline your ponycar.

Police the area around your Mustang before you take that picture. Pieces of trash in the foreground will ruin an otherwise beautiful composition.

Photograph your Mustang from many angles, literally "around the clock", which means, to get the right sun angles, you'll have to alternately move the car, keeping the light behind you, or to the side. Shoot these pictures high and low, don't make them all from eye level. That's why pros carry a small step ladder. And sometimes you will have to lay down on your back to get an impressive low angle of your Mustang.

On many shots, fill your picture frame with as much of the car as possible. Don't compose a picture where your Mustang looks like "an ant in a shoebox".

Shoot plenty of vertical shots, don't make them all horizontal. Cars are horizontal, but magazines use a vertical format.

Give some of your pictures life by including people. Have them doing something — maybe raising the top, checking the oil, washing the whitewalls, waxing the hood, adjusting a rear spoiler, installing a tape stripe.

Take some detail shots of your Mustang as well as the full views. Focus in on the interesting parts of your car — an insignia, hood scoop, gas cap, etc.

If you really get energetic, you may want to try for some action photos. I like these! For "flash-bys", set your camera on 1/30 second, and "pan" your Mustang as it zips-by (40 to 50 MPH is fast enough with the 1/30 shutter speed). It helps to have a tripod, however, to keep your camera level with the plane of the car. The idea is to photograph your Mustang with as sharp an image as possible, and blur the background to get the impression of movement. A little haziness or blur of your car is okay, and sometimes desirable, however, to give a clear impression of speed. Also, since your wheelcovers are spinning, they will also be fuzzy.

Another way to show speed is to photograph your moving Mustang from another moving vehicle. Set your camera at 1/30 or 1/60 second, and shoot. In this instance, you definitely want your Mustang as sharp as possible, because there is no relative speed between you and your Mustang, and the idea is to blur out the foreground and background.

If you own a performance Mustang, it's nice to have some pictures of it "leaning" into or out of a curve. You don't need a slow shutter speed for this type of shot, just good positioning and/or a telephoto lens.

For engine shots, you need a flash. Even when your meter reads enough available light for an exposure, the final print will show dark areas that the flash would have illuminated. But don't flash an engine which is partly in sunlight and partly shadowed. Take it to a more evenly lighted area, and then make use of your flash.

Unless you are shooting the interior of a convertible with the top down, you also need a flash to light-up those dark areas inside the car. A wide angle lens is very convenient for interiors, since you are working in tight quarters. From the middle of the back seat, you will be able to focus and get the whole dash into one shot. If you really want a picture of your car's interior, but you have a ripped bucket seat, for example, you can have somebody in the seat to hide these imperfections. It's a handy technique. You can even apply it to other areas — hands on a steering wheel to hide a crack, or feet over a tear in the carpet.

The cardinal sin — photographing the shady side of the Mustang. Almost all of the side detail is lost in the shadow.

Another cardinal sin — signposts, telephone poles, and other objects "growing" out of the Mustang's hood or roof. Also, watch out for unattractive signs, cars, buildings, trash, etc. in the background.

Here's another example of the photographer's shadow falling onto the subject; in this case, the engine compartment. Changing the angle of the Mustang would have eliminated this problem.

Ah, that's better. Sunlight and fill-flash together can create a beautiful, detailed engine compartment photograph.

For a different perspective of the Mustang, shoot from high and low positions. Many professional photographers carry a step-ladder on assignments, but a tree or a pick-up truck will work just as well.

How To
PREVENT MUSTANG THEFT

by Jim Smart

You've had a great evening. You and your best girl or guy have just seen a great movie, and there is magic in the air with that "nothing can go wrong" feeling that goes with the part. You gather your belongings and head for the parking lot. You're ready to bail into your "baby" for the nice drive home.

Suddenly, the passing thought, "Where is my Mustang? I know I parked it here next to this Volkswagen!" A frantic search of the parking lot confirms one thing — the painful truth — your Mustang is missing. What should you do? You have little time for tears, though they come anyway. You've lost not only an expensive piece of property, but your best buddy as well.

First, call the Police. Provide the responding officer with every detail, covering every little nick and scratch, plus the items that make your Mustang different from the rest. Leave no stone unturned in assisting the Police; the more you provide, the better the odds.

Now, what can you do yourself? Of course, keep your eyes peeled (we know that you will) and check your local wrecking yards and used car lots. Watch the "classifieds" in your local newspaper, as well as newspapers from neighboring cities. Make this a daily event. Should your year and body style Mustang turn up for sale, go look at the car as a prospective buyer. If, by some lucky fate, the car is yours, leave a deposit (expressing intent to buy) and return later...with the Police! The serial number may have been changed, but there are still many ways to identify your Mustang. The original serial number can be found in more places than just the driver's door data plate and the left inner fender. Serial numbers are also stamped into the right inner fender, hidden beneath the outer fender skin. Other tell-tale signs, like special options you added yourself, always help to prove ownership. More on this later.

The next step in your search is to contact Police departments in every city in the U.S.A. and Canada. By yourself, this task is impossible, but you do have help in the form of local and state Police. Teletypes and All Points Bulletins can be transmitted to thousands of Police departments within hours. Then you'll have law enforcement officials all over the country providing assistance in recovering your Mustang.

Next, contact U.S. Customs. They control all ports of entry and, in your case, exit into and out of the United States. Everyday, automobiles are stolen and exported to foreign countries to be sold at sometimes *five* times their U.S. value. False papers are fabricated and the car is out of the country within two days! Once your Mustang finds its way into another country and is titled there, chances of recovery are slim. Titles aren't even required in some countries, in which case the whereabouts of your Mustang will never be known — except to its new owner.

Inform the vast number of Mustang and Shelby clubs that cover North America. These clubs are there to help you. You can help them by providing extensive information about your stolen Mustang, including photos.

After performing your "homework", keep an Eagle Eye on the local roads and stay in constant contact with the Police. About every two months, write once again to the Mustang clubs to hold their interest in your problem. Persistence is the key to recovery.

TYPES OF MUSTANG THEFT

Earlier we mentioned visiting the wrecking yards, and here's why. Many stolen automobiles fall victim to the Chop Shop Boys who steal the car, then disassemble it within hours; in many cases, right in your local neighborhood. Chop Shops aren't widely publicized, but thousands of cars vanish each year, only to be stripped and crushed. You may say, "Oh, it'll never happen. My Mustang is too mint. They would sell it whole." Well, let me burst your bubble. In the eyes of the auto thief, your baby represents dollars, and they have no respect for its beauty and condition. Used parts, and Mustang parts in particular, bring big bucks and thieves know it. Chop Shops are a multi-billion dollar business, although 100% illegal, and many people make a living at it. Chop Shops range from very private "under-the-counter" sales to that wrecking yard just down the street.

Other forms of theft vary. Your sporty Mustang may look real appealing to a kid out looking for a fast evening or a way to impress his friends. If the key was left in the ignition, you really opened a can of worms. Your Mustang will be worse for wear when the Police finally find it. You may luck out and find it parked somewhere with only your Fleetwood Mac tape missing — or the Police may find it wrapped around a telephone pole.

Another "biggie" is just plain auto theft where the Mustang is stolen, retitled and serial numbered, usually repainted, and sold. In most cases, the poor car is moved to another state, retains the same serial number, and is retitled. Steal-To-Order automobiles are available for those with big bucks.

PREVENTION

The ultimate prevention against theft, of course, is a locked garage. For some of us, that is not always possible and the garage won't be with you at the movie theatre, so you must resort to an arsenal of anti-theft ideas. Various burglar alarms are available at a variety of prices. They vary from your economical "shaker" alarms (which work quite well) all the way up to rather expensive "door and shaker" systems. The more expensive alarms include their own "yelper" sirens, much like Police and ambulance sirens, which are more likely to attract attention.

"Page" alarms are a recent innovation. They work silently and only you know that the Mustang is being tampered with. When the alarm sounds on your personal beeper, you have several choices of action: You can go to the Mustang and catch the individual yourself (not recommended in these days of slayings and violent crimes), or you can call the Police. You may wish to observe the thief's actions from a safe distance while waiting for officers to arrive. The major drawback with the "page" alarms is their distance range. If you're more than a mile away from the car, the alarm signal may not always reach you. But the manufacturers are improving the product, so keep them in mind.

Another anti-theft device, the kill switch, can be as unique as your imagination. The switch can be mounted anywhere to prevent engine start, even if hot-wired.

HORSE THIEVES

Roger Waddle of Topeka, Kansas, dropped off his 1966 Mustang hardtop at a local body shop last February for body work, but when he got the car back, the body work was a bit more extensive than planned. Thieves stole the Mustang from the body shop parking lot, stripped it, and left the remains on a frozen pond hoping that the pond would thaw and the Mustang would sink. Fortunately (or unfortunately, depending on how you look at it), a truck driver discovered the hulk before warmer weather arrived. When recovered, only the tires, frame and rear fenders remained.

"This is indicative of a chop shop," said Topeka Detective Jim Gilchrist. "Because of the car's value, the parts were more valuable than the car in one piece. Someone who knew what he was doing cut that car. It was not an amateur job."

All major parts had been stripped from Waddle's Mustang: gone were the front fenders, roof, engine, transmission, doors, grill, trunk lid, chrome trim, and most of the windows. Even the identification numbers had been removed, but Waddle identified the car by stickers in the remaining windows and the ignition switch.

In a 1980 bulletin, the FBI described a chop shop as "...a facility that disassembles stolen autos for purposes of selling parts. The illegal parts business annually grosses an estimated $4 billion tax free."

A fuel shut-off valve or relay is also effective. The shut-off valve is manually operated, and can be installed directly beneath the driver's floor where the two fuel lines join. The electrical relay type is solenoid-operated by a hidden switch. In either case, with the shut-off valve closed, the thief can start the car and drive off, but he won't get very far before the carburetor runs out of gas and the engine stalls. More than likely, the thief will become discouraged and scram.

To aid the Police before the fact, install personal identification plates in various unseen areas of your Mustang. Fabricate approximately five 4x3 inch metal plates and stamp or etch them with both your Mustang's V.I.N. number and your Social Security number. Affix the plates in assorted locations: beneath the carpet and insulation, in the rear seat coils, down in a door, behind the rear panels, or any other well-hidden spot. If possible, rivet the plates to their location, using a silicone sealer between the plate and steel components to prevent corrosion. You can also etch the information into frame members and the floor pan. Then record the information, including the plate locations, and file them with your title. Hopefully, you'll never need the information.

This article is not meant to scare you or give you a phobia about driving your Mustang. Indeed, it is meant to educate you on the hazards associated with the everyday operation of your Mustang, and what you can do to prevent disaster in case the "unthinkable" happens. Each day that fear runs through our minds; it is up to you to prevent it from becoming a reality.

Do you know where your Mustang is tonight?

How To
BUY A USED MUSTANG

by Steve Leake

FOR SALE: 65 Mustang Conv., 6 cyl., 4 sp., new paint, EC. $4600.

For weeks the only recreational reading you've done has been the newspaper classifieds. You've got Mustang fever really bad this time, and you think the above ad may be just the prescription for your cure.

Is it a steal or a rip-off? Every Mustang shopper has faced this dilemma. How can the buyer, particularly the first time buyer, know if this car is a fair buy? The experienced Mustanger would want to know more about what lies beneath that new paint, and whether that four speed is a stock "Dagenham" before buying.

While there is no substitute for experience, the lessons can prove costly and frustrating. It's better to learn from someone else's experience if possible. Why don't you tag along with me while I shop for a used Mustang.

WHAT ARE YOU LOOKING FOR? WHY DO YOU WANT A MUSTANG?

At first glance the answers to these questions may seem self-evident, but they will simplify your car hunt 100%. Do you plan to buy a car for its resale potential? Perhaps it's a show car that you want, or simply reliable transportation. What model and year are you interested in? What options? If you fail to seriously address these issues

you will be comparing apples to oranges. My local Mustang market ranges from $500 to $9,000 for a bewildering array of coupes, convertibles, T-5's, fastbacks, GT's, and Shelbys, original stock to highly modified. You need to maintain a clear image of what you want to avoid floundering on the rocks.

Keep these general guidelines in mind: If you are buying a car to resell, shop for one that requires cosmetic work only. Major mechanical repairs are always more expensive than you figure. If you intend to restore your car for show, plan to spend thousands of dollars (four to six thousand) on the restoration project. With these kinds of costs after you buy, seriously consider stealing the car to keep your total costs down. In addition, try for a unique car, a GT perhaps or a model that will insure a high value relative to your restoration costs. Remember, it costs almost as much to rebuild the suspension on a six cylinder coupe as it does on a Hertz Shelby. If your aim is transportation you will have no trouble finding a good buy. Look for dependability and low price.

Now for the big question? Do you have the skills and tenacity to do most needed repairs yourself? Do you know how much money you will have to spend making that car into what you envision? (See side bar on page 94 for typical Mustang repair costs.)

The typical buyer would be better off paying top dollar for a car that has everything fixed by the previous owner.

It is rare that the seller can charge enough to recoupe his costs, so the buyer saves money in the long run by not having to make those expensive repairs. Of course, this does mean that your initial cost will be considerably higher.

Two years ago I bought a 65 fastback for $1400 with the thought of restoring it for daily use. I finally realized that I would be into it for $5500 in order to make it exactly what I wanted. Very few buyers would be willing to pay that much if I decided to sell. So unless you like to do the restoration work, you are better off paying a higher initial cost, and saving on those expensive repairs.

In order to buy a Mustang, you first have to...

LOCATE THE MUSTANG MARKET IN YOUR AREA

Mustangs are everywhere and it won't be hard to locate the ones for sale once you learn how. If your car hunting activity is limited to newspaper ads, you are needlessly shortchanging yourself. Looking for a good car is like job hunting. The real demand jobs are rarely advertised. People seek them out and apply for them long before a newspaper ad is placed. Owners of rare Mustangs are always hounded to sell. They don't have to place an ad to find an interested buyer, so you must become familiar with the cars in your area. Here are a few ways of picking up the scent: 1. Talk to the parts person at your local Ford dealership. 2. Contact

91

any local club of Mustang enthusiasts. 3. Find out who in your area does Mustang restoration work. They will know of potential cars on the auction block. 4. Mustang shows are an excellent source of clean cars. Just don't expect to steal one for a low price. 5. Other owners. One of the best sources of information is word of mouth. Most Mustang addicts can't resist eyeballing a pony with a "For Sale" sign draped around its neck, so let your friends do your looking for you. Even my non-Mustang friends are constantly telling me about their uncle or son-in-law who has this "rare" Mustang parked out back. Check these leads out 6. I have saved classified advertisements for last, largely because they are the most traditional way to locate autos, and to reinforce my earlier warning that many of the best cars are sold without ever getting into the paper.

Look at cars that are seemingly out of your price range. There are a couple of reasons why I think this is good advice. First, by looking at the expensive Mustangs you will develop a standard of comparison useful when you come back to your price range. You will know what your money can buy relative to the cost of fixing a lower priced car. Second, my experience as both a seller and buyer has taught me that when the price of a Mustang goes over $3000 the telephone calls become much more scarce. One acquaintance who sells a lot of Mustangs views $3000 as a psychological pivot point for the buyer. He swears that he can sell a half dozen clean three speed coupes for $2800 for every $3800 GT coupe he sells. The seller may well get nervous and chop his price if the phone stops ringing.

Before we leave the subject of classifieds, I want to alert you about the common practice of using the word "restored" when, in fact, only hasty cosmetic repairs hide the obvious flaws. You just don't buy a restored car for $2500...well hardly ever...there's always that *one* car.

DO YOUR HOMEWORK BEFORE SHOPPING

The excitement of car buying is in looking over all of those fine Mustangs. However, there are a few things that you should do before you hit the streets. If financing is needed, take your hat in hand and see your banker before shopping. If you locate a good buy, there will probably be several buyers in line, and the car will go to the one who produces the cash first. Despicable as it sounds, I have heard of sellers who reneged on deposits, and sold to higher offers that came along later.

It is also important to "know your Mustangs". After seventeen years, those little changes made by a succession of

Mustang shows are always a good source for exceptional cars. Just don't expect any bargain.

Don't laugh. I considered buying this one, but the owner wouldn't budge enough from his stated price of $1000. A four speed GT with no rust. In addition, the engine compartment had already been detailed, a thankless job facing every restorer.

owners can take a toll on the value of the car as an investment (if that is a concern). Two useful publications are the "Mustang Recognition Guide" and the "Mustang Value Guide". Not only are they enjoyable reading, but they will help you spot alterations which would not be obvious to many buyers. The price is cheap compared to what you will save by buying "right". The Value Guide is the closest thing to a "Blue Book" on Mustang values. Once you determine the condition code for the car and add in the value of the options, you can obtain a ball park dollar value for the car.

MUSTANG SHOPPING KIT

In addition to your reference books you will find it useful to pack along

some of the following items:
1. A measuring tape to check for spring sag.
2. A pair of spark plug wire pullers to avoid electrical shocks while checking engine condition in the manner explained in a later section. A well insulated glove will do just as well.
3. Test equipment such as vacuum and compression gauges.
4. A small floor jack and jackstand will be useful for checking front end parts and brakes.
5. A magnet for determining the density of plastic body fillers. You know that you have struck "Bondo" when your magnet suddenly loses its attraction to metal. A keen eye for sheet metal distortion will usually suffice, but the look on a seller's

face when you pull out your magnet to critically review his new paint job is worth the price of the magnet. Just be sure to protect the paint by keeping paper or a thin cloth between the paint and the magnet.

6. A camera, particularly a Polaroid, may prove valuable if you plan to look at several cars.

A CHECKLIST KEEPS YOUR MUSTANG FEVER IN LINE

The biggest problem facing most Mustang buyers is one of their own making. They want to buy a pony car so badly that they are often overwhelmed by one or two positive features and neglect very costly defects. A young friend phoned me one night to exclaim over his new car, his first Mustang. All he could talk about was the sound system. He was so overwhelmed by the graphic equalizer and quad speakers that he neglected to note such consequential defects as a bad front end, (it took both hands to keep the car on the road), a leaky slipping transmission, and burned valves. The body would have been okay if the trunk had not been caved in or the wheel wells flared by crowbar.

The best way to insure against turning into jello over that pony interior or four speed is to have a definite plan to follow when inspecting each car. The Mustang Value Guide includes a scoresheet for appraising cars. I expanded upon it to come up with my own detailed checklist which covered every conceivable item of importance. It proved invaluable by reminding me to try those window mechanisms, electrical items, check that weatherstripping, etc., the kinds of things easily overlooked when in the grips of full blown Mustang fever.

There is an additional benefit to using an appraisal form or checklist; you can show the seller the basis for your offer. Too often the seller sets his price by looking in the classifieds to see what others are asking. They are likely comparing their tired old coupe to a fully restored 100 point coupe, and not realize the very real difference in value.

MECHANICAL CHECKS FOR THE NON-MECHANIC

If you like a car well enough to consider making an offer, you can improve your bargaining position by knowing something about its state of repair. I will describe some simple but revealing tests that you can do on the spot.

ENGINE: The engine balance test is a quick way to check general engine condition. First the theory. In an engine, each cylinder should carry a portion of the workload. If you put that

Your Mustang shopping kit. With just a few basic tools, and the all important references, you can learn a lot about a car.

cylinder out of action the performance should suffer *if* that cylinder was doing its share. The balance test consists of listening to the engine run with all cylinders firing, and then disconnecting a plug wire with your plug wire pullers or by hand with an insulated glove. If the cylinder was functioning properly, there should be a noticeable miss or drop in RPM when put out of commission. Check each cylinder in turn, but don't forget to reconnect the one that you just checked. If there is no noticeable miss or change in RPM, there is either an internal problem in that cylinder like burned valves or worn rings or the plug is not firing properly. The wire or the plug itself could be bad. Check the wire by holding it near the block. You should get a healthy blue snap when the engine is running.

A spark plug inspection will help judge engine condition. They should not have black oily deposits or carbon build-up. Pull the dipstick and look for signs of water and low oil conditions. If the Mustang has an oil gauge, watch where it registers *after* the engine has

warmed up. One with bad bearings can show good pressure when cold, but will bottom out once the engine warms and those clearances open up.

Inspect the radiator. About half the cars I looked at were low on water. Look for a good mixture of water and anti-freeze. If a car is losing water the owner is not likely to refill it with $4.95 per gallon anti-freeze; he'll just add water.

DRIVELINE: A good clutch should engage smoothly, without chattering or slipping. Bring the car to a full stop with the front wheels against an obstacle such as a curb, shift into high gear, and with a slight revving of the engine release the clutch. If the clutch is good, the engine should stall and die. If it doesn't, then the clutch is probably slipping.

A close relative to the clutch, the throw-out bearing, should be checked too. It is only a $10 item, but the labor to get to it can eat into your budget. Check its condition by idling the car with the transmission in neutral and your foot *off* the clutch. Listen carefully to all the sounds that the car makes. Then depress the clutch and listen again. Do you hear any difference? A worn or out-of-adjustment throw-out bearing will make some noise, usually a whirring sound.

A transmission should shift smoothly and transmit power without clunking or delay. A whining sound from the rear end could indicate a failing differential. Check the automatic transmission fluid. Is it full? Is it red? How does it smell? Slipping transmission bands can cause a burnt odor and a color shift from cherry red.

Take a long hard look at the suspension since old ponys have a reputation for being swayback and somewhat weak in the knees. Those squeaks coming from the front end may be warnings that the "A" arm bushings are due for replacement, an expensive undertaking at most shops. To determine the condition of the ball joints and wheel bearings, jack up the front end until the front wheels clear the ground. Grasp the tire at the top and bottom and try to rock the wheel. There should be no movement.

Tire wear patterns will also reveal any problems in the front end. Just be sure to check the rear tires too since the tires may have been rotated five minutes before you drove up.

If you feel unsure of your ability to uncover front end problems, take the car to a tire store and have it put up on the rack. Ten or fifteen dollars can buy lots of peace of mind.

Rear springs are notoriously weak on early Mustangs. Look for booster springs and air shocks, two common remedies for sagging springs.

Beware of oversized tires. There is little room for extra rubber under early Mustang wheel wells. A little hard cornering and a fast dip or two will quickly reveal any rubbing on those oversized sneakers. Again, the common cure seems to be booster springs and air shocks. Removing these to restore your car to stock condition is no problem, BUT you will be dismayed when you have to shell out an unexpected $500 for new tires because those big ones kiss your sheet metal everytime you ease over anything bigger than a BB.

INSPECTING THE BODY AND PAINT: With a little practice, you can detect most problems in this area. Be sure to inspect in good light and get low to view the sheet metal and paint from all angles. Keep in mind that light colors are very forgiving of ripples and flaws. Give extra scrutiny to that new white paint.

If the car has been repainted, look to see if the color matches the original paint. Check for overspray on trim, weatherstripping, and springs. Look for flaking and peeling around those "hard to reach" places like emblems and other

trim. Surface preparation makes a paint job, but that is precisely where the cut-rate shops cut their costs. You may even ask the seller for a copy of the paint work order. It will describe the type and extent of any body repairs.

Use the information from the identification plate to check on the authenticity of the Mustang.

When looking for rust in a Mustang, go straight to the trunk. Most damage seems to occur in the wells where water can collect and rust out pinholes through the quarter panels. Since most of my experience has been with California cars, I have been spared the sight of rotted floor pans, so common in the East. Don't forget to open and close all doors, hood, and trunk lids. Try the locks, keys, radio, etc. Use that checklist.

When buying a Mustang, I would rather buy one with warts and all,

without any covering of new paint. I want to see how sound the metal is. If the body is straight, this car may be your best buy because the worn but tough original finish makes a much better foundation for a quality paint job than a softer repainted surface. There is a psychological advantage too. Sellers are inclined to lower their price because of faded and chipped paint, but usually demand a premium if they've had it repainted, no matter how poorly.

HORSETRADING (NEGOTIATING A DEAL)

Finding a Mustang that meets your needs is one thing, but you still have to pry it loose from the owner at a reasonable price. Most of the cars I encountered were overpriced by four hundred to fifteen hundred dollars. On the other hand, some were actually underpriced by almost a thousand. So relax, because some "steals" are still out there, just not as many as there used to be. Everyone in America seems to know someone who "sold one of them little cars for six thousand dollars".

Sellers fall into two basic categories: There is the casual owner who has owned the car for years, and may even be the original owner. He may not know very much about Mustangs in terms of their infinite variety and values, but enough bargain hungry Mustangers have tried to separate him from his pink slip that he is going to set a healthy price on his car.

Then there is the...ENTHUSIAST. He wears Shelby T-shirts and carries

TYPICAL MUSTANG REPAIR COSTS

Ball joints and control arm bushings	$250 to $300
Rear springs	$200 new & installed $150 re-arched
Transmission Automatic	$250 exchange $45 + parts for rebuild. You remove.
Four-speed	$325 exchange $45 + parts for rebuild. You remove.
Engine (Complete rebuild. Labor not included)	$800 for standard V8 $1500 for a modernized high performance.
Exhaust system (duals)	$200
Paint job (costs vary widely)	$500-$3000. Body work will hike the price considerably.
Replace a quarter panel	$500 per panel
Interior (Installed) Carpets	$150
Headliner	$140
Seat covers (Pony)	$325
Door panels (Pony)	$325
To change wheels and tires	$400-$500

dog-eared copies of MM publications. He can recite in detail each style of radiator cap ever used in each production year. He too may set a high price, but I think that the psychology and strategy for dealing with each type is not that much different. In both instances, display your knowledge of Mustangs. Enlighten the casual owner regarding Mustangs and their values without being overbearing.

If the price is totally out of line, the seller will soon realize it. Never feel embarrassed about offering less than the asking price. Show the seller how you arrived at your offer so he will see that you are not trying to rob him, or are likely to pay more than the car is worth.

Never deride the type of repairs or alterations that the seller has made. This is just a simple matter of courtesy, and is my personal pet beef with buyers when I am selling a car. If you don't like something about the car either offer less money and fix it or simply don't buy.

While admiring the car, innocently inquire or note what extra parts are scattered about the garage. Later, if negotiations stall, you may suggest that the seller sweeten the pot by tossing in that "Cross Boss" manifold, air conditioner, or...? The seller will still get the cash price he wants, and you will get more for your money.

Once you find a car at a fair price,

buy it. Don't make the mistake of driving too hard a bargain and lose the deal to someone else who is not as interested in wringing blood from the seller. Don't lose any sleep over whether or not you could have knocked the seller down another hundred dollars.

When selling a car, I can smell a serious buyer. There are a lot of people "looking" at Mustangs, so you want to be perceived as a "buyer" if you want your offer to receive serious consideration. When a casual looker asks me if I will take "less" I tell him no. But, when a man is standing there with his checkbook open, I am going to give it a bit more thought.

Be prepared with a cash deposit when you make your offer. Nothing aggravates a seller more than to have what appears to be a solid buyer back out. Other callers have been told that the car is sold or an ad may have been cancelled. Recognize this nagging fear on the seller's part, and be prepared to stake your deposit as security that you'll come through. A lower but firm offer and deposit may well beat out a higher but "shaky" offer.

Don't discount the possibility of using your present car as a trade, particularly if it is another Mustang. A seller surprised me with just such a proposal. He had a custom Hi-Po GT fastback for six thousand dollars, too rich for my

blood...until he proposed to take my 65 pony as a three thousand dollar trade. Suddenly, I was looking at "expensive" Mustangs instead of those strictly in the $2500-$3500 range.

One parting piece of advice: don't give up just because a seller has rejected your offer. Check back with him once a week and leave your phone number. He may get tired of running $40 classified ads and accept your offer. To demonstrate my point I made phone calls to the sellers of all the cars on my list a month after looking at them. Several had sold, but many hadn't. A $4000 convertible sold for $3300 and a 65 fastback took its asking price of $2500. I later learned that it had been on the market earlier for $3500. The rest are still available and could very well go to a persistent buyer who manages to catch the seller on a day when he is willing to give the car away.

Probably the most important thing learned during my "buy of a lifetime" search is this: they're a lot more common than you think. Several times over the past few years I have come across such exceptional buys that my stomach would knot up and my brain race at night conceiving financially irresponsible ways to pull off the purchase. Each time it was a "once in a lifetime" opportunity too. Now I realize that they pop up pretty often...if you're looking.

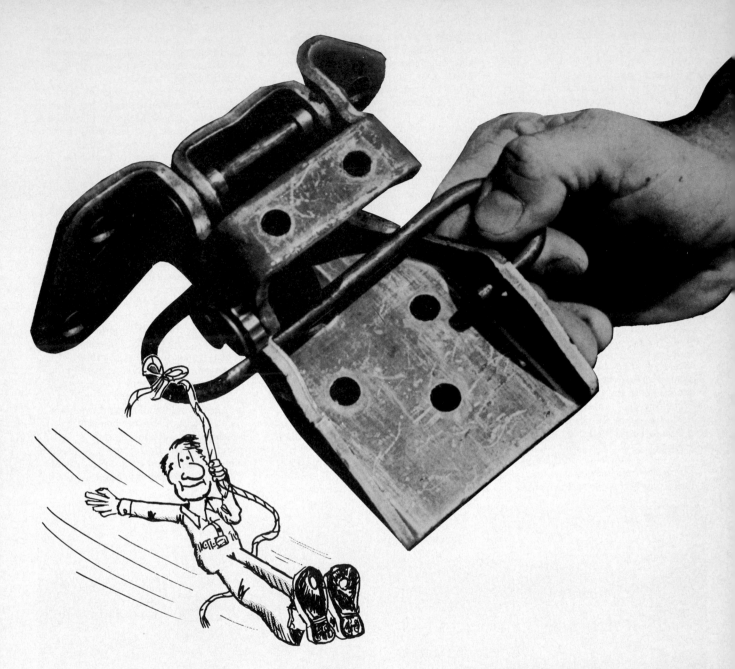

How To
REPAIR MUSTANG DOOR HINGES

*Slam the door
on your
hinge problems*

by Donald Farr

Door hinges, those creaking, popping and annoying hunks of metal that keep your Mustang's door attached to the car, are possibly the most tolerated pieces of equipment found on the Ford Mustang. You know them by their springs that jump out of place and their spine-tingling "Pop!" that accompanies every door closing, mainly on the driver's side. You even lift up the door so it'll latch properly.

But you don't have to. Replacing a door hinge (or hinges) is a basic bolt-in operation, requiring only a few hand tools and an extra helping hand. Many do-it-yourself Mustangers cringe at the thought of removing the door, and then realigning it later, but the actual removal/installation process is amazingly simple and the realignment steps require only a bit of patience.

When Pete Geisler, owner of Pete's Lacquer Shop in Orlando, invited

MUSTANG MONTHLY to participate in a door hinge replacement on his 1968 hardtop, we jumped at the chance to witness the operation first-hand. Pete made it look easy, completing the job in less than an hour.

Many lower door hinge headaches are caused by the hinge spring; in '65-66 Mustangs, the coiled spring will actually jump out of the hinge. "Replacing the spring alone will not always prevents a future reoccurence", says Pete. "In most cases, the hinge will have to be replaced for a permanent fix".

Mustangs use 2 hinges for each door, but the lower one supports most of the door weight and is usually the culprit when a problem arises. Pete replaced only the lower hinge in his Mustang, but the upper hinge, if required, can be replaced at the same time.

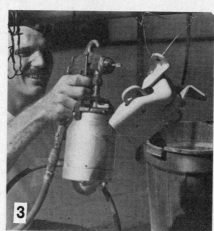

1 - Check the condition of your hinges by having a helper wiggle the door. Worn hinges will wobble, and should be replaced.

2 - The First Generation Mustangs used 4 different door hinges for each of the body style eras: '65-66, '67-68, '69-70, '71-73. Pete's '68 has a newer-type rod spring when compared to the older '65-66 coil spring.

3 - For appearance and rust prevention, the replacement hinge should be painted before installation. Pete sands the hinge lightly with sandpaper, then applies a thin coat of primer before spraying the paint. Some hinges are coated with a protective substance which must be removed with a solvent before sanding. Paint the hinge the same color as the car exterior.

4 - Five to six bolts attach the door to the hinge, depending upon the model year. Support the door's weight with a floor jack or blocks and have your helper steady the door. Unbolt the door and store it in a safe location.

5 - Each hinge fastens to the door post with 3 bolts. The lower hinge usually wears out before the upper.

6 - A small ratchet makes the bolt removal easy. Earlier '65-66s require a 9/16" socket; later years need a 1/2".

7 - At the factory, the hinges were installed before the car was painted, so a sealant was applied to prevent water from getting behind the hinge and creating Mustang enemy Number 1 -rust.

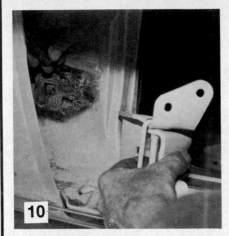

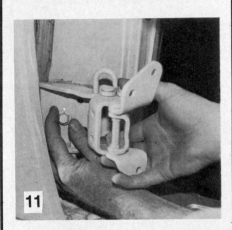

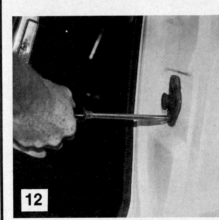

8 - A certain amount of rust will have formed behind the hinge anyway, and should be scraped off along with the old sealant.

9 - Spraying some grease onto the hinge area will help prevent further rust and also lubricate the hinge for easier door adjustment.

10 - The hinges actually bolt to a movable plate within the door post. Position the plate with a Phillips screwdriver or ice pick. Occasionally, the plate will slip out of its brackets and fall into the door post. In that case, the kick panel can be removed to retrieve the plate.

11 - Position the new hinge into place and reinstall the bolts. Don't tighten the bolts completely. Recaulk around the hinge with 3M 8531 Heavy Drip-Check Sealer. If you're just replacing one hinge, loosen the other in preparation for the door adjustment. Before reinstalling the door, tape the edges of the front fender and door to prevent nicks in the paint. With your helper supporting the weight, bolt the door to the hinges.

12 - Pete removes the striker plate before beginning the door adjustment. That way, he can check the door-to-body clearances without latching the door and altering the door position.

13 - Patience is an asset when adjusting doors. Some will fit the first time, others require more trial and error. With the hinges still loose, estimate the door position and tighten the bolts. Close the door slowly and inspect the fit. If you're off, loosen the hinge bolts and reposition the door. Keep trying until the door fits properly. If you really want to get specific, your shop manual includes exact door gap specifications. Once you get the correct adjustment, tighten the bolts and reinstall the striker plate.